Praise for *A Leader's Guide to*

How fortunate to find Judy Brown's notions, learnings, and reflections on transformative leadership all in one place for easy access in her new book, *A Leader's Guide to Reflective Practice*. Judy weaves together leadership theory, models and metaphors in a clear, sharp and practical integration, using her unique capacity for congenial conversation. Judy's vibrant work on the nature of leadership is an illuminated manuscript of spirited practices that help leaders be more systematically effective and holistically human using the creative power of dialogue, and reflective lived experience.

Irene McHenry, Ph.D.
Executive Director, Friends Council on Education

Judy Brown brings an astonishingly well read and seasoned mind to this book. It is filled with solid reflections on the purpose and practice of being not merely a "good" leader, but more importantly, a "transformational leader" – one who promotes successful humans as well as successful organizations. *A Leader's Guide to Reflective Practice* offers a compendium of field tested ideas that have been honed in the fire of authentic and reflective poetry. By honoring the human spirit, she points us toward the kind of perspective and wholeness necessary for any organization to both nurture and flourish.

Michael S. Glaser,
Poet Laureate of Maryland,
professor and former academic administrator.

∞

I've seldom read a book so rich in both spiritual guidance and practical help. Brown's wise advice is distilled from years of experience – and her poetry is a gift to the soul.

Betty Sue Flowers
Poet, Editor, Educator, Business Consultant and
Director, LBJ Presidential Library and Museum.

As a long-time devotee of Judy Brown's work, I think this book is her best. *A Leader's Guide to Reflective Practice* reveals both the depth of her experience in the complex world of organizational leadership and the simplicity that lies on the other side of complexity. This alchemy of complexity and simplicity yields wisdom, which is what you will find here. And "A Leader's Guide" has it all: honest engagement with the demands of leadership; a compelling case for the necessity of reflection; guidance on modes of practice so diverse that anyone can find a reflective path here; and stories and poems that serve not merely as grace notes but as openings into new ways of seeing and being. I commend this book to any leader who wants to serve well by staying grounded in the realities of the world and the soul.

Parker J. Palmer
(author of "A Hidden Wholeness," "Let Your Life Speak," and "The Courage to Teach")

If the ideas of leadership practice draw you in, then this book is important for you. The disciplined prose punctuated by the shorthand power of poetry brings together the intellectual, emotional and spiritual in a masterful way. The plain English grounded practice descriptions, and personal notes allow you to embrace its wisdom and go beyond where you are. A combination of practical examples and the emotional shorthand of poetry forms a powerful "one-two punch" on your thinking. This is a very satisfying book.

Dr Roger Saillant.
President and CEO of PlugPower,
an alternative energy company.

∞

A Leader's Guide
To Reflective Practice

Judy Brown

∞

Note for Librarians: A cataloguing record for this book is available from Library and Archives Canada at www.collectionscanada.ca/amicus/index-e.html
ISBN 1-4251-0445-2

Portions of this book have been Published previously. I appreciate the permission to Include them here.

PUBLISHING™
Offices in Canada, USA, Ireland and UK

Book sales for North America and international:
Trafford Publishing, 6E–2333 Government St.,
Victoria, BC V8T 4P4 CANADA
phone 250 383 6864 (toll-free 1 888 232 4444)
fax 250 383 6804; email to orders@trafford.com
Book sales in Europe:
Trafford Publishing (UK) Limited, 9 Park End Street, 2nd Floor
Oxford, UK OX1 1HH UNITED KINGDOM
phone +44 (0)1865 722 113 (local rate 0845 230 9601)
facsimile +44 (0)1865 722 868; info.uk@trafford.com
Order online at:
trafford.com/06-2202

10 9 8 7 6 5 4 3

Appreciations

Thanks to everyone who has been part of my cross-sector, cross-institution, cross-boundary leadership work over the past decades--those who have joined me in dialogues, classes, and retreats, and all forms of rich conversation.

Thanks to those whose voices are in the stories that follow, and those whose actions and words have prompted the poems. You are legion and you are my teachers. I am grateful for your wisdom.

Thanks to the colleagues who encouraged me, and goaded me and pushed me to put the words on paper that now make up this book. I send appreciation, too, to the communities of practice of which I have been a part: The James MacGregor Burns Academy of Leadership, The Shambhala Institute for Authentic Leadership, the Center for Courage and Renewal, and The Society of Organizational Learning

To all those who might read these words that follow and make good use of them in the world, my gratitude for the bridge you are building to greater understanding and wiser action--and for carrying the work forward into worlds I can only dream of.

A special appreciation to those who have taken time to read manuscripts and to make wise suggestions, especially Margie Hagene and Linda Wolfe.

∞

And warm, rich appreciation to my family for their interest in and support of my wide-ranging, zig-zagging work in the world--my children Meg, Ethan and David--my brother David who as a builder of wooden boats is a constant inspiration to me--and my husband David who has been the heartbeat and the discipline behind making the idea of this book a reality.

To each and all, my thanks.

Judy

∞

Table of Contents

∞

∞

Several of the poems and other materials in *A Leader's Guide to Reflective Practice* have been published in some form previously. I appreciate the permission to include them in this collection.

∞

8
Wooden Boats

I have a brother who builds wooden boats,
Who knows precisely how a board
Can bend or turn, steamed just exactly
Soft enough so he, with help of friends,
Can shape it to the hull.
The knowledge lies as much
Within his sure hands on the plane
As in his head;
It lies in love of wood and grain,
A rough hand resting on the satin
Of the finished deck.
Is there within us each
Such artistry forgotten
In the cruder tasks
The world requires of us,
The faster modern work
That we have
Turned our life to do?
Could we return to more of craft
Within our lives,
And feel the way the grain of wood runs true,
By letting our hands linger
On the product of our artistry?
Could we recall what we have known
But have forgotten,
The gifts within ourselves,
Each other too,
And thus transform a world
As he and friends do,
Shaping steaming oak boards
On the hulls of wooden boats?

∞

Welcome

At the heart of the reflective practices that lie within this book, is an invitation to shift the initial conditions of our inner territory – to reset the beginning spot of our thinking, our feeling and our spirit, in order to open the way to action that has greater vitality, sustainability, grace and life.

As I share these practices, and my poetry, I feel as if I am inviting you into my living room, for a relaxed, longish conversation-- about things that matter to us. Not a conversation about cabbages and kings. But rather a dialogue about leadership and heart and ways of caring for the world we see around us.

So these are words of welcome, meant to open a space for an exploration together.

I imagine us pulling comfortable chairs around a fire in the fireplace. Someone is playing the piano. Folks are helping themselves to coffee or tea. Some people are looking out the plate-glass windows at the huge old oaks. A few moments of silence. A candle lit. And then we begin, speaking one at a time. Together we weave a conversation about how as leaders, we are able to stay in balance and in touch with ourselves, so that our actions in the world are apt, are wise, are all we would want them to be.

We are leaders in different ways. Some of us hold the formal title of leader in one or another organization. Perhaps a business. Or a school. Some of us lead by teaching. Some of us lead by the way we live. As one of my students once said to me after a semester of exploring these ideas, "I realize that leadership has nothing to do with title. It is a way of life, a way of being in the world."

And how did we end up in this living room, together? We have been brought together, perhaps, by our curiosities, and our need for renewal. Like a two-year-old who has gotten too wound up

∞

for his own good, who has overstepped some boundary, we are grown-ups needing a "time out."

There have been many "time outs" in my own life as a leader, a writer, a teacher, a poet. Moments of reflection. Time to think. Sometimes long periods, sometimes short. Sometimes the reflection comes in the very time of action. And sometimes it has been a weaving or perhaps a dance, between the times of being an active (some would say driven) leader, holding responsibility for organizations, for initiatives, for the output of teams. And other times of stepping back to explore and teach ways for leaders to keep themselves grounded and aware in the midst of the flow of their leadership work.

In this book, those times have come together, for me, and I hope for you, as well. It is here in the world of exploring dimensions of the leader's inner processes, in threading through our thinking/feeling life, the life of spirit, that the relationship of the inner to the outer becomes clearer to us, and the resources of the inner become more naturally available to the work in the outer world. We do that individually, but we also do that collectively.

And the collective exploration, the dialogues and rich conversations, create a chance for us to share those practices, so we feel less alone in the world. We share so that our leadership responsibility becomes a shared experience, like a fishing net we hold together, rather than a solitary boulder we push up solitary hills in our solitary way--as is so often the felt experience of leadership.

Here, together, in the spaces of these pages, as you read, we explore the practices that leaders can use in order to stay alive to their inner resources, and to be able to tap the full instrument of themselves--to practice what I think of as "full band-width" leadership.

∞

There is science in this conversation--science, and art, and poetry, stories, and philosophy, and guidance, suggestions, things to experiment with. Questions to sit with. To consider.

The experiences that you bring to this gathering of minds, all that runs through your mind as you explore these pages, that too is a part of this reflective process. There's a fair amount of white space in these pages, particularly around my poetry. Write there. Draw there. Sketch there. Make your own notes of your own wisdom and wondering about reflective practices, your ways of stepping back and learning from your own life. It is that learning that in the final analysis, makes our life our own, and makes it rich with meaning, connecting it to the things that truly matter most to us and to our service in the world.

Welcome.

Judy

∞

Fire

What makes a fire burn
Is space between the logs,
A breathing space.
Too much of a good thing,
Too many logs
Packed in too tight
Can douse the flames
Almost as surely
As a pail of water can.

So building fires
Requires attention
To the spaces in between,
As much as to the wood.

When we are able to build
Open spaces
In the same way
We have learned
To pile on the logs.
Then we can come to see how
It is fuel, and absence of the fuel
Together, that make fire possible.

We only need to lay a log
Lightly from time to time.
A fire
Grows
Simply because the space is there
With openings
In which the flame
That knows just how it wants to burn
Can find its way.

∞

13
Leadership and Reflective Practice

If the world of a leader is the world of action, why are we exploring reflective practices, the quiet inner world of the leader, the world of thought and feeling, the world of dialogue and conversation? It turns out there are many good reasons to do so. And it doesn't hurt to trace those reasons as we begin our exploration together.

Research on leader behavior suggests that reflection, especially for highly successful action-oriented leaders and managers, is counter-intuitive, requires disciplined and intentional practice to become a solid part of a leader's development strategy, and is critical to success.

- Chris Argyris in his HBR articles, "Teaching Smart People How to Learn" and "Double Loop Learning in Organizations" notes how leaders, particularly those that are very smart and very successful, develop personal routines or reactions to any feedback that challenges their view of themselves as a very successful executive. That "learning disability" makes it hard for them to learn from experience. Organizations can develop a similar learning disability.

- The Ladder of Inference, from the work of Chris Argyris provides a theoretical model for how individuals select and screen data and how experience itself increases (rather than decreases) the chances we will cut ourselves off from critical information. Argyris's work suggests that inquiry into the perceptions of others and curiosity about our own thinking, enables us to "walk ourselves back down the Ladder of Inference" and come to

∞

understand, and reconsider, the hidden assumptions that block our learning. It also increases the likelihood that we will actually "see" critical data that has been falling outside of our perceptive range.

- Umberto Maturana, in his book *The Tree of Knowledge,* notes that the perceptive process by which we know something is true, comes only 20% from our taking in information that "is out there" (that is data from the world that is processed by our eyes) and is 80% the result of our making associations and assumptions from our prior experience. This makes us very vulnerable to misreading what is going on.

- *Cone in the Box* from my dialogue work at the Center for Creative Leadership is a visual that helps us see the partial nature of our information and helps us turn toward strategies for both holding onto our point of view and inquiring about and accepting seemingly contrary data, thus creating a more complex understanding than the appealing simpler one we may cherish. It is a critical idea in dealing with complex, conflicted and dynamic systems. It helps us explore unexpected and seeming inexplicable difference.

- Thomas Kuhn's classic book *The Structure of Scientific Revolutions* shows how even scientists treat as irrelevant ("noise in the system") data that doesn't fit the current scientific view of how things work. Like the scientists, we ignore the "noise" in the system that is inconsistent with the "theory in practice" that drives how we operate.

∞

- Peter Senge and his colleagues in *The Fifth Discipline Field Book* have coined the term, "Systems Thinking" which is the disciplined exploration of what might be going on in complex cause and effect loops with time delays. Without the ability to take in data without judgment and without deletions, it is hard to create a realistic systems map of what is happening.

- Tara Bennett-Goleman in her book *Emotional Alchemy* combines an understanding of the story-line the individual holds that is shaping her response to difficulty, with an understanding of how personal reflective practice can help one see in ones processes what once was completely unperceivable.

- Ron Heifetz in *Leadership Without Easy Answers* points to the human tendency toward what he calls "work avoidance" in order to avoid coming to grips with the anxiety-producing realization that the usual response is of little value in the current dilemma. When our current circumstance challenges our very way of understanding how the world works, we are in the presence of an adaptive challenge, one in which the leader needs to provide guidance, direction and protection, as the organization learns its way into a more effective response. In *Leadership on the Line; staying alive through the Dangers of Leading* he further explores the importance of processes and relationships that allow us to get honest feedback on our performance. Heifetz calls this process of reflection "getting up on the balcony" where instead of being caught up in the dance, we can reflect on the patterns of movement.

∞

- Neustadt and May in their classic book *Thinking in Time; the uses of history for decision-makers* note the tendency of leaders to select inappropriate historical analogies which make a case for what they want to do. We may make the same mistake in terms of our own history, as we seek experiences from our past to help us make sense of our current experiences.

- Bill Perry and other learning theorists remind us that significant increases in learning require support and challenge both, and in high doses. It takes discipline to challenge ourselves and it takes courage to receive feedback from others that challenges our ingrained view of ourselves. Robert Kegan's book *How the Way We Talk Can Change the Way We Work,* opens with Bill Perry's words: "Whenever someone comes to me for help, I listen very hard and ask myself, 'What does this person really want—and what will they do to keep from getting it?'" To what lengths will we go to avoid learning what would make it possible to have what we really want? Now *there* is a powerful question.

- From the work of the Harvard Negotiation Project, the wisdom of the book *Difficult Conversations* shows us that difficult conversations represent disagreement over what happened, over what meaning to ascribe to what happened, and most importantly they represent a threat to our self image, to our cherished beliefs about ourselves as individuals. Difficult conversations are difficult because they require seeing ourselves as less than perfect, or as different than the perfectly competent

∞

human being, good and caring parent we want to believe we are.

- Peter Drucker in a classic HBR article *"Managing Oneself"* makes a case that self-understanding (accurate knowledge of ones strengths and weaknesses) is the key piece of knowledge that a good leader needs. He argues that our attention should go to maximizing our talents, as there is greater pay-off in that than in trying to do what we are not good at. And the first step in maximizing our gifts, is a clear, honest appraisal of those strengths seen from the inside out.

The goal of reflective processes and attention to inner dimensions of leadership is to maximize the leader's capacity for learning from experience and to create a personal leadership norm for intentional (and often counterintuitive) learning. Reflection (though it may seem to slow us down) serves to amplify, speed and deepen learning, and it creates the capacity and the instinct to maintain a practice of reflecting on experience over a life-time, individually for you as individuals and leaders, and for the system in which you serve. The value is therefore equally on your experience (the action) and your reflection (learning).

Why seek new ways, alternative ways, to reflect?

To achieve greater insights and learning, we need individual and collective routines that maximize our learning, which broaden the range of ways we learn, and which break through the natural human habits that can wall us off from many of life's lessons. Whatever our present habits and preferences for reflection, they are by themselves likely insufficient to the task, particularly if we are quite successful individuals. We get stuck in our successful and limiting ways of learning.

∞

So why shouldn't we just reflect in the way most natural to us?

Most of us prefer to learn in certain ways. If I use myself as an example, I have to admit that I learn best by doing, by talking, by writing–not by solo research, not by games, not by role-plays. So I am resistant to those other kinds of learning which could challenge me in new ways and make it possible for me to see things that are out of my current line of sight. I prefer journal work and dialogue so it is very easy for me to get "stuck" in the world of words. I have to strategize to get myself out of the "word" habit.

Because our natural preferences are limited, it is helpful, therefore to seek out practices that allow us to try all kinds of "learning" processes, thus expanding our capacities and increasing what we are able to absorb. By watching our own attraction to one form of reflection, or our resistance to another, we learn important information about ourselves. Last summer, for instance, I got dragooned into playing a role in an improvisational theatre production. I was terrified, yet I learned a huge amount. I have historically been particularly resistant to "playful" processes for learning (such processes challenge my view of myself as serious) so it is sometimes hard for me to enter into playful processes for reflection, and I often am shy to offer them to others whom I see as equally resistant because I fear they will think I am not serious.

Why vary our reflection strategies?

- We each have only certain sources we trust for learning (I trust the wisdom of close friends, and the books of certain authors); and we are often absolutely averse to teachings from certain people (for instance, I have trouble taking in information from people whose politics are radically different from my own). It is interesting to ask what we gain by having certain methodologies and certain

∞

people that we can't learn from. My worst personal case of this was a boss I came to dislike tremendously and therefore could not learn from. Because there seemed no other alternative for me, I left the organization. By my inability to be able to learn from this individual, I had narrowed my options considerably. From that experience I have learned to ask myself whenever I think someone has nothing to teach me, "What view of myself that is sacred would I rather hold in place than allow that person to be a source of learning?" That rude question usually shakes me loose of my stubbornness. So I suggest we seek practices that open us to learning from a wide range of sources thus increasing our learning and our options.

- We may be part of a work culture that holds the belief that it is unique and cannot be compared to any other unlike enterprise, and therefore cannot learn anything useful from other professions. That belief on the part of individuals in a profession, or a work culture, creates a significant learning disability. Therefore practices that promote cross-boundary and cross-profession learning and reflection are helpful in breaking that habit and compensating for that disability.

- All of us are limited to roughly 180 degree vision—that's why there's 360 degree feedback in many organizations. The notion of 360 degree feedback suggests the value of listening to the perceptions of those who look at things that we cannot see—either because of our role, our defensiveness, our experience or our professional training.

∞

- Any one approach to reflection/learning is in itself limiting because it accesses only some of the variety of data we need in order to make wise decisions. And left to our own devices, most of us will stay in our comfort zone about how (if) we reflect on what has happened, and why. There are many models that explore those preferences and those differences: the Myers Briggs explores preferences for intuition, sensing, thinking, feeling; the learning styles inventory of David Kolb, explores preferences for experience, for reflection, for theory building, for experimentation; the NLP model explores the dominance of visual, auditory and kinesthetic learning; Carol Pearson's work helps us see the narrative structure we use for making meaning of our life experience. These are just some of the very useful models. In each model we learn that we have particular preferences. Experimenting with and practicing a range of reflective practices can help us balance and expand out from our own preferences. For instance, I have a strong preference for intuition rather than sensing as a way to take in information. The journal work I do helps me begin to track sensing data more effectively, to be more observant and noticing of detail data. The journal practice broadens what I take in. And the walking meditation of "What I see is this......and the story I tell myself is this.....and what I also see is......and another story I might tell myself...." is a practice that breaks the hold of intuition (with its preference for story) over me, because it shifts me back and forth from story to data.

- We over-learn some things. Like a cat who has stepped on a hot stove, we learn to never go near a

∞

stove again, even if it's cold. Of course, we under-learn other things: for instance, if we are not self-confident, we may be unable to recall all the times we have been successful at new undertakings. Trying alternative ways of reflective learning can increase our perceptive capacity. I have considered myself to be a cautious person, not particularly courageous, although others might have said different of me. My experience with the Outward Bound high ropes course a few of years ago changed my view of myself in important ways. It also changed my capacity to learn from physical experience. So new data got in, and the experience also changed the operating system by which I made sense of that data.

- Without reflective practice, we overlook what works for us. Like many leaders, I am so sensitive to feedback about how to change and improve that I lose sight of what does not need improving or changing, but is working beautifully already. Reflective practice that puts in place an automatic, disciplined debrief of events and experiences, so that we are collecting regular data all along, increases our ability to understand what is already working, and it puts in perspective the areas that do need improvement.

- An automatic process for debriefing any event is the logic behind the After Action Review process that the Army uses as a regular discipline for learning. Being able to take in complex reality and quickly learn from it is a challenge to individuals and organizations. All organizations and cultures have some learning disabilities. And disciplined broad-ranging reflective practices are necessary to

∞

compensate for those inherent learning disabilities. The After Action Reviews (AARs) create a structure and discipline for an honest focused learning conversation irrespective of rank. And that structure is used whether an event is a "success" or "failure." From the point of view of learning, it is neither success nor failure. It is just an event, full of potential learning. This quote, framed, sits on my bookshelf: "There are no secrets to success. It is the result of preparation, hard work, and learning from failure." Colin Powell. These reflective habits are not necessarily natural to the military, to its structures, nor to its personnel. The structure of After Action Review is designed to broaden and extend the natural reflective/learning processes of the organization and the individual leaders, by "breaking" some of the usual rules, like the supremacy of rank.

A willingness to experiment with unusual ways of sorting out thinking, of reflecting can offer real breakthroughs. I was a very reluctant leader of an offsite where the financial business folks wanted to experiment with balancing peacock feathers as a way of understanding the importance of keeping ones eyes on the prize, on the bigger picture. Under duress, I led 600 "numbers folks" in a balancing exercise that produced real breakthroughs for them and has continued to produce breakthroughs in other work cultures. I have learned to be surprised.

Similarly, I thought the notion of writing a "letter to the self" at the end of a learning experience was hokey, but having tried it am startled how much people appreciate having a letter show up in their mailbox six months after our work together, in their own handwriting, reminding them not to forget critical insights. And now I do a letter at the same time they do, and find the unexpected mail similarly helpful.

∞

And as a final observation about reflective practice, I would note that perhaps the greatest resource for reflection is the power of a good question, one which places us in a genuinely open and curious mind-set, and invites fuller exploration of what is going on. I have my own set of such questions, ones that I have happened on, and others I have created, over time and I am happy to share them with you. Yet developing such a list for oneself is perhaps one of the most important leadership reflective practices. So feel free to use those that follow as a starting point for creating your own set.

∞

No Seed Grows

No seed grows
Except by
Breaking through
Its own
Protective coat.

∞

25
Thought-Starters for Encouraging your Own Deeper Learning

- What I'm noticing is…and what surprises me is….

- What I think is going on is…but if the opposite were true then….

- What's hardest for me is…and if it were easy….

- What I usually do in this kind of situation is…and what I notice about the impact of that is….If I were to do the opposite, what would probably happen is….What stops me from doing that is….If it no longer stopped me, then….

- The limit I would most like to break through is….

- If I were ten times bolder, or a hundred times bolder, then….

- If I were being tougher on myself what I would say is….If I were being more compassionate with myself what I would say is….

- The part of me that is my best self wants me to….

- If I knew what I did would be on the front page of the New York Times, then what I would do is….

- The part of me that I don't want to hear keeps telling me to…Why is it so hard for me to listen to that voice…what would happen if I took that voice seriously?

- If truth were my friend in this I would….

∞

- If the difficulties that plague me in this were a test of my future leadership capabilities, my strategy for passing the test would be to....

- If this challenge were in my path as a gift for my leadership development, something to place me on a path to even greater service and achievement, its most important lesson to me would be...and I would respond by....

- What I notice is...and the story I tell myself is....What I also notice is...and another story I might tell is....

- I have experienced similar challenges when....

Stepping Back

Stepping back
Creates the space—
For insight,
Some small flame
Of creativity,
For some new
Sprout
To push through
To the light.
The growth will
Do what's needing to be done;
Our work is to
Create the space.

∞

Questions for Encouraging Deeper Learning in Another Person:

- What are you noticing? What about that surprises you?

- What do you think is going on? What if the opposite were true?

- What's hardest for you? What if it were easy?

- What have you historically done in similar situations? How has that worked for you? What approach would be its opposite?

- What limits would you like to break through?

- Tell me how you would change this if you were ten times bolder, one hundred times bolder?

- What if you were letting yourself off too easily?

- What would your best self want you to do?

- If your actions were to be on the front page of the New York Times, then what would you do?

- If there were a part of your own wisdom that you didn't want to hear, what would it be saying to you? And why is it so hard to listen to?

- If truth were your friend in this, what would you do differently?

∞

- If the difficulties that plague you in this were a test of your future leadership capabilities, how would you go about passing that test?

- If this challenge were in your path as a gift of your leadership development, something to place you on a path to even greater service and achievement, what would it be trying to teach you? How would you want to respond?

- What data are you seeing, and what story are you telling yourself? What other data is present? What other story might you tell yourself?

- Where in your life have you encountered similar challenges?

Hummingbirds Asleep

When do the humming birds
Get naps? When do they sleep?
The tiny helicopter-birds,
Buzzing about their busy business
All day long are nowhere to be found
At four fifteen
With dawn an hour away.

When they're at rest, they're gone.
Evaporated. They don't exist.
It's only busyness, activity
Gives them their visibility,
Their realness in our eyes.

Maybe we think the same of us.
Without our work,
Activity,
We disappear,
Or so we fear.

∞

The Lessons of the Iceberg:
Working below the Waterline

I have been struck by the way transformational leaders take time to see into their own processes, to disclose their feelings and thinking, to be honest about themselves, their train of thought, their thinking, their reservations and struggles. With that leadership courage, the transformational leader invites all of the human talents of us all, and the result is a new and necessary richness in our world of work, a sense of being at home, ourselves, in the workplace. And it is that process that creates the transformation, the elevation of energies, vision, capacities to a new level.

Now I want to take us a step further in that exploration about being a transformational leader, to ask, "What can a leader do to increase those dimensions of self-awareness, and thus to lead wisely through times of uncertainty? How can we tap the highest aspirations and talents of those around us, and aim all our sights on a higher plane of service and of effectiveness? Are there practices that help us make a difference in the world whether we are a leader by title, or simply one who wants to make the world a better place?"

The answer is "Yes, there are practical next steps," and yet the starting point is a quiet place of reflection. Why are leadership personal reflective practices critical to the world around the leader and within the organization? Why be reflective when the world needs action? What is the logic, the pay-off, for stepping back from the action from time to time?

A simple answer: Reflective leadership practices focus our attention on the level where leaders have the most leverage, and which most impacts their action: the space of thinking and

∞

feeling, the stories we tell ourselves about how the world operates, the unwritten rules of culture.

Working below the waterline of the iceberg

The world in which we lead is like an iceberg, with only the tip of it seen above the waterline. That tip is represented by events. Everyone is watching the tip because it's visible. Yet most of the iceberg, as we all know, is below the water line. And below the waterline are the dimensions of our life and organizational life that are shaping what we can see above the waterline.

1) **Events:** The transformative leader (and any leader) is faced with events, anticipated and not anticipated. Since we're talking about icebergs, let's use the sinking of the Titanic as an example. On her maiden voyage the Titanic struck an iceberg in the North Atlantic and sank. That was an event.

Each of us can no doubt think of major "events" in our work world. Huge surprises, some good and some bad. You know how much attention they grab.

2) **Patterns of Behavior:** But level two of what a transformative leader is aware of, and working with, is patterns of behavior that lie just below the surface. We can only see them if we look below the visible events, below the waterline. How did patterns of behavior contribute to the Titanic hitting the iceberg? Everyone accepted the captain's supremacy. Those on the bridge ignored the detailed notes in the log book about multiple reports of sighting of icebergs with the location of each carefully noted. Passengers and staff ignored the shortage of space in the life-boats for all 2000 people on board.

∞

THE ICEBERG

Deference to expertise, to position, to authority–all were patterns of behavior imbedded in the culture of the time. Such patterns of behavior are imbedded in all organizations—some push the organization in directions that are very productive, and others clearly hamper the organization.

3) **Structures:** At a third level on this "iceberg" of reality, are conscious and unconscious structures and rules that contribute to the pattern of behaviors, that produce the "event". Back to the Titanic: these structures would include rules about running the ship full speed ahead no matter what in order to make it to New York on time. Rules that the way you avoid icebergs is by having a "look-out" watching for them

In your own organization, what are structures that are important? Powerful? That keep things operating in certain ways? For good or for ill?

4) **Mindset:** And finally there are mind-sets, ways of thinking that had created the structures, that produced the patterns of behaviors, that resulted in the event. So we might say that a train of thought sank the Titanic? Perhaps. Here are some of the mindsets at work that night: The Captain believed that ships the size of the Titanic were literally unsinkable. Everyone seemed convinced that expertise and experience were ample insurance against disaster and since the Captain was taking his final voyage in a long and successful career with the company, they had plenty of experience on board.

You can probably think of mindsets, trains of thought that shape how things are done in your work world. There may well be important ones that you so take for granted that they don't even come to mind.

∞

It is at this level of exploring and shifting mind-set, that the leader has the greatest potential for transformation. Mindset shows up individually and collectively as a train of thought, a dominant story of how things are, how the world operates. Sometimes we are aware of those mind-sets and other times they are so ingrained that we are almost unconscious of them.

Reflective leadership practices give us increasing awareness of mind-set, our own and others, so that we are increasingly able to bring to consciousness the images, the stories, the ways of thinking that are shaping the structures, that are patterning the behavior, that are producing the events and our reactions to the events.

Thus transformative change begins in the depths, at the very bottom of the iceberg, only the tip of which is action and event. Transformative change begins in the depths within the leader, and then with the leader's capacity to help the organization explore the depths of its own thinking, understanding, story. A change, a shift at that deeper level, changes everything up the line.

There is often little leverage in trying to anticipate events and avoid them, or in tinkering with the after-effect of events. Yet many leaders spend huge amounts of time doing just that. With their attention captured by events, their calendars jammed with activity, they are unable to place their attention at the level within themselves, and around themselves, where real transformation can begin.

Practices for getting below the waterline

The obvious question, then, is "How do we get to that depth?" Here then are twelve ways individuals can explore the richness of the depths of mindset, intentionally and regularly, to become more aware of the shape of our thinking, as part of a transformational leadership practice of reflection.

∞

1) **Reflecting on the iceberg:** This reflective process pulls us back from fixing the symptoms, and reacting to the events around us. As a leader it helps us practice getting some space to think more deeply about what is going on around us.

Think of a particular vexing incident or event. Using the "iceberg" structure discussed above, detail what you noticed at the level of action/event. Then write down the various patterns of behavior that seemed to contribute to that event. Then note the various structures in the organization, culture, or situation that produced those patterns. And finally, detail as many "mindsets" or ways of thinking as you can, that built the structures, that produced the patterns and that caused the events.

2) **Leadership shadow:** This practice gives us a chance to observe, without judgment and without need for action, a leader who approaches things differently than we do.

Identify a leader whom you admire, whose approach is different from your own. Arrange to spend a day "shadowing" that leader, observing what they do, how they do it. If possible conclude the day with a half hour interview of the person. Ask how they think about their own leadership, how they handle the management of change, what they consider their greatest gifts and their greatest legacy.

3) **Steppingstones:** Steppingstones is an exercise for stretching perspective that is helpful when you are starting a new project or a new phase of work or when you are feeling overwhelmed by tasks and demands.

Take 15 minutes of quiet time to answer this question in writing; "What are 6 or 8 steppingstones, events, choice-points that have brought you to where you are in your work and your life?" Just write down what comes to mind. Then note what stands out for you in the list you have made. Are there surprises? Patterns?

∞

I find it helpful to go through this process every few months or so, as my perspective on my own life and work often shifts, and those shifts produce important insights that impact my leadership.

4) **Easel art:** This is an exercise for shifting out of words. This process can be effective in exploring our vision for our work in the world, our life-time calling. It can also help when one is confused, conflicted, uncertain, intense, disoriented, or anxious.

Directions: Using newsprint or flipchart material as an artist's canvas, with big colored magic markers begin simply drawing, scrawling, sketching, scribbling—whatever comes to you. Only rule: no words. Work until you are tired. Leave the "art work" over night. The next day, stand before it for 5 or 10 minutes and then name it and date it.

5) **Genius level questions:** This practice shifts us from trying to find the answer to asking more powerful questions.

Practice asking completely open and curious questions, questions that only the other person can answer, and about which you can have no possible theory. For instance, you might ask a colleague what they are most excited about in their work…and what gives them the greatest worry about it. Or you might ask someone who is wrestling with a problem, whether they've ever encountered anything like that before in their lives. And in written form, you can turn this process on yourself, asking completely open questions about whatever is vexing you.

6) **Visual explorer:** This practice shifts us from words to images and visuals as a way of thinking about a dilemma.

Directions: Create your own collection of pictures or post-cards of all kinds. Spread them out on the floor. Keeping in mind the dilemma that you are wrestling with, walk among the pictures,

∞

and notice which one seems to attract your attention.   When you have picked a picture or perhaps two that seem to speak to you, sit with the picture and take some notes about it. What attracted your attention to it? Is there some way that the picture might have wisdom for the situation that you are struggling with?

7) **Accessing physical wisdom**: As your interest in reflective practice grows, make a commitment to engaging your physical self in some process that creates new "understanding" within your body. It might be taking up golf (or improving your game), walking a labyrinth, taking a high ropes course (which I did after I was 50 and terrified of heights), setting off on a canoeing river trip, taking up dancing, kayaking, skiing, gardening, woodworking. Pay attention to the subtle awareness that is part of that physical practice.

8) **Nature's teaching**: This practice is helpful when we have run out of ideas for resolving a particular problem or dilemma.

Take a long, slow walk in some natural setting---a path by a stream, under the trees, in a park. What in the natural world attracts your attention?

Perhaps it is a particular tree. Or a clod of dirt. A pine cone? Or a stone? A squirrel? One particular leaf?   A sheaf of pine needles?

In silence, observe the object for an extended period of time. What do you see after a while that you didn't notice at first? What do you know about the life-cycle of that object? What might the object suggest to you about your dilemma? How does nature, generally, respond to what you are facing?

9) **Immerse yourself in imagery**: This is practice that helps us sink into the richness of language that is metaphorical rather than direct. It increases our capacity to hear the images in the life of our organization, as well.

∞

Find a poem that appeals to you. (Two good sources of poetry are Garrison Keillor's *Good Poems*, and *Teaching with Fire* edited by Sam Intrator and Megan Scribner.) Note words or phrases that stand out for you in the poem. What do they suggest to you? About your life? About your challenges? About your gifts?

10) **Daily writing**: This is a practice that helps us listen to our own inner wisdom, to take in the lessons of our own lives. It also helps develop greater awareness of our thought processes.

Set aside a period of time each day and write freely, from wherever you are in your thinking and feeling. Your writing may reflect what now stands out for you about yesterday, or the sense you have of the day ahead of you. You might begin thus: "This is a time in my life when…." Or "Today, no matter what happens, I want to make sure I…." Let your life speak to you. What questions is it asking of you? What information is it giving you?

11) **Who draws your best energies**: Think about people in your life, over your lifetime, who seem to have drawn the best out of you, in whose presence you were your best self and were able to really do fine work. Make a list of those people. What do they have in common, if anything? How often do you now place yourself in the presence of such people?

12) **Harnessing creative capacity**: Each day take a moment for some creative endeavor. Cooking. Writing bits of poetry. Playing music. Singing. Sketching. Painting. Building something. These processes rest our thinking mind, place us in flow state, and provide important perspectives for seeing the world around us in new ways.

∞

Some concluding thoughts:

As you experiment with these twelve personal practices and others you may learn from colleagues, note any shifts in your awareness, your centeredness, your sense of purpose. Are you aware of things you didn't used to notice as a result of one or another of these practices?

Why does all this matter? Because it contributes to your effectiveness as a leader. It increases your capacity to lead change, to be transformational. When you ask people to talk about the best leaders they have worked with, people who lifted them and the organization to new heights, almost always they will mention the leader's extraordinary capacity to listen, to be present to others, to see the possibilities in others, to hold an unwavering vision. As leaders, we can't do that for others, without practice, and that practice begins within ourselves. Reflective practice is a core transformational leadership skill. It helps us see, and then shift, the deep thought processes and mind-sets that shape transformation in the outer world. The roots of transformation in the world around us, lie in the deeper work within us.

∞

It is the Small Space

It is the small space
In our lives,
The daily corner
To which we need repair,
That can create a
Whole new world.
For us,
Vast,
Unconstrained,
And opening.

∞

If it is Difficult

If it is difficult
Try something
Different.
A tiny shift
Might find
The easy
Natural path,
The one
That's meant
To be.
Persistence
And insistence
May be
Good things —
But not always.

∞

Journal Writing as Reflective Practice

Years back, at a particularly difficult time in my life, when I was casting about for a way to sort through my own confusion and struggles, a friend suggested that I try the structured journal developed by Ira Progoff. Progoff, a psychologist, had developed a process for working with what he called "the material of ones life."

I was feeling unusually mired in confusion both personally and professionally, in a kind of tangled bramble patch of life. My mother had recently died, I was emerging from a divorce, and I was ending a highly visible and prestigious fellowship experience with no clear idea of what I wanted to do next, except that I didn't want to go back to where I had come from. I was a high energy, high achieving Type A, at sea.

Partially out of trust in my friend's judgment, and partially because I had no better idea at hand, I bought Ira Progoff's book *At a Journal Workshop*, and signed up for his weekend journal workshop.

What I remember of that weekend workshop with Ira is sketchy but important to me. I remember being given a rather conventional black loose-leaf notebook with lots of paper and section dividers for different kinds of writing: "daily log," "period log," "dream log," "dialogues." I remember thinking it a novel idea that people could write in silence and privacy in a room full of strangers, and could feel supported but not intruded upon by each others presence. I remember being startled that people who felt moved to read from their journal material could do so, could be openly emotional about it (heresy for a small town mid-westerner like myself) and could be listened to without comment or judgment, their words received but neither judged nor analyzed. I recall Ira sanctioning utter silence and unlike my

∞

usual sociable self, I practiced utter silence the entire weekend. I remember beginning to understand that it didn't take an expert beyond myself for me to make sense of a good portion of my life. It simply took my own disciplined attention to my own experience and my own words. I needed to absorb my own experience and take it seriously.

I was surprised at the impact of writing in the different sections of the journal. Within those structures I began to see things about myself, and learn things from my own life, that were much more provocative and interesting then when I wrote in the "dear diary" style I'd developed as a teenager keeping a journal, or when I just mused (or agonized) within my own head about my life, or when I read books written by wise authors, or even when I talked with thoughtful friends.

These journal structures had very different properties than my usual ways of trying to make sense of life. They resulted in new insights and greater compassion for myself. They also increased my ability to envision a path forward. It occurred to me that several dimensions produced those outcomes:

- •Writing rather than just thinking, seemed to give my words greater solidness;
- •The surrounding uninterrupted silence created space to explore;
- •The sentence stems opened up new ways of thinking particularly the sentence beginning "This is a time in my life when ...."
- •The sense that all of us were in this together gave support and a legitimacy to the journal work.

I also remember the impact of Ira's quiet presence, as if without words he somehow convinced me that it was legitimate "work" to spend time with my own thoughts and words. I don't remember anybody I met that weekend. Except Ira. And myself. I was particularly drawn to the idea of "Steppingstones," Progoff's term for those major events or choice points that have brought us to

∞

where we are in our life. I came home from the weekend and spent an entire day with a garden trowel meditatively edging the stepping stones in front of my house.

Over the next few months, I moved through the difficulties of that time of my life with the help of the journal. I used dialogues with people no longer alive, dialogues with work, dialogue with my body, somehow letting each "speak" to me in the writing on the page. That process allowed me to get unstuck. I made professional decisions that would open new worlds to me. I formed my own business working with organizations in the midst of change. I was out and on my own in many ways.

But those changes, and the journal as a guide, turned out to be temporary then. Soon I fell in love and found myself in what would be a relationship of many years. I was recruited back into a university, to a business school where I developed programs for executives. It was work I loved and once again my consulting practice became something I did on the side. I became a parent, first of two lively stepsons in their teens, and soon after my 41st birthday, to a daughter.

The journal somehow got lost in the process, perhaps because my own understanding of the value of personal inner work within community was too fragile for me to sustain within a family unit where I was the only "journaler." Perhaps I was afraid that the privacy of the journal would not be honored, and that the children would find their way into some of the "material of my life" not meant for their eyes. I also sensed that my husband saw the journal as secrecy and a waste of time (an assumption that I never fully checked out) and that it strained our relationship. The simplest explanation for setting aside the journal was time: I was a woman in my forties, with a hard-charging career, a household with teen-agers, an infant daughter, a lively golden retriever, and responsibility for aging parents. There just wasn't time to keep a journal. So I told myself. It didn't occur to me then that the

∞

journal was not an addition to the responsibilities I felt, but rather a way to navigate them with grace. I would learn that later.

But even as I set the journal aside, I had perhaps unconsciously taken to heart some of its disciplines. I found myself drawn to more dialogic communication processes, which I began to integrate into my work. I became known professionally for my dialogue work with groups and I began to receive increasing numbers of requests to help struggling and conflicted leadership teams engage in a quality of conversation that often opened new avenues of healthy understanding and development for them. And as the challenges of back surgery, and the illnesses of three aging family elders, as well as a very difficult professional period piled up on me, I was eventually driven back to the journal, in a response not unlike that which Parker Palmer describes as being a "contemplative by catastrophe."

This time, I was less drawn to the formal dialogue structures and I relied instead on the simple daily journal and the dream log. I began writing daily, religiously, every morning upon rising. If there would not be time, I would get up earlier. And in addition to the journal process, I walked before the day started, before the day had a hold on me. Walking and writing served as linked meditative processes tying the journal to the natural world and the world of the physical. I walked in the snow. In the starlight. At dawn. Day in and day out. The beauty of the walk and the comfort of the journal allowed me to claim my life and my self back from the arenas to which I had unthinkingly given self away. I began to see I had unknowingly squandered my spirit. I was reclaiming self from a world of agonizing overwork, from losing myself in motherhood, in marriage, in to-do lists. No one had forced me to live that way nor would have even wanted me to. I had simply slowly lost myself in the responsibilities of my life.

∞

Now, before anything else had a claim on me, the journal had a claim. I was meeting myself again, much as I had with Ira, a decade before. My understanding of the journal deepened although I never returned formally to the guidance in Ira's book, *At a Journal Workshop*. I simply drew on my memories of the process and used what seemed most useful to me in the moment.

I think it was the experience of the journal, and its support for what the Quakers call "the inner teacher" that made beginning to attend Quaker meeting a natural development in my life. My husband and stepsons were products of Quaker schooling and attending Quaker meeting became my first experience with a religious tradition since I had become a "lapsed Methodist" after graduating from my small mid-western high school. Quaker meeting with its silence, simplicity and no minister, was quite different from my childhood experience with the more formal liturgy. The meeting, with its long periods of silence from which people spoke only when moved to speak, carried an echo of Ira's journal process. Like the journal discipline it required being with the material of one's life, letting what the Quaker's call the "inner teacher" speak to us, and sometimes sharing the message of that teacher. Other times not.

For four years, I sat in silence in Quaker meeting, saying nothing, listening to what others had to say. Thinking. Daily I wrote in my journal. I logged my dreams without comment or analysis, and read them as if they were stories told me by my subconscious. My early training in literature made that a natural way to hold dreams, just as it had made dialogue a familiar structure earlier on. The journal was a place to take in and digest things that were important to me—experiences, poems, readings, stories people told me, beauty, even pain. And it was a way to take my own experiences and words seriously and to see the progress, the movement in my life.

∞

I wrote my way through changes of all kinds: a professional set-back, the launching of my independent practice once again, moving our family back to the Washington area, the death of my father. It was out of the pages of the daily log that began to emerge the beginnings of a book about the end of my father's life and my reflections on loss and learning. Then, unexpectedly one summer day a single poem showed up, in the journal, as if dictated:

> And we will sell no more
> of our eternity
> in payment for dead dreams,
> for the denial of our losses.
>
> But we will speak of loss
> and of rebirth,
> and we will treasure
> gifts which are our own . . .
>
> This know we now and always.
> Let the earth remind us
> when the storms around us
> overwhelm the tiny still voice of truth within.

That poem was like a single thunderclap before a storm. I recognized it as a personal truth coming from some deep inner space. My words in the journal switched back to prose. For almost a year. And then came torrents of poetry.

> That one year
> came a single poem
> in the summertime,
> a voice of power
> that I recognized
> from far away
> as mine,
> a single poem
> like a thunderclap
> before the rain

∞

of poetry that came,
months later,
water to a desert
in my heart,
refreshing me,
making me whole again.

Now I lived almost daily with this strange experience of watching my journal words shift from prose to poetry and then back to prose. Having learned from Ira and from practice to not judge what I was writing, and by now having bit by bit gained comfort and fluency with my own words and writing, I simply wrote down the poems as if I were taking dictation.

What I noticed though was that while the prose entries in the journal explored what I intended to explore, the poetry had a mind of its own—it went where it wanted to, and clearer, faster, deeper—with many surprises. In a period of five years I wrote hundreds of poems, many of them completely finished as they emerged on the journal page. Un-editable. Within those poems was news from my inner terrain that rang utterly true for me, words that even I could not ignore. Often a poem would be the first indication to me of important feelings, insights, or conclusions that in earlier years I would have denied or ignored. No longer so.

I was beginning to see that the power of the journal went well beyond the writing itself. It seemed to me that the journal process was part of a call to lead a life "divided no more," a life in which various inner practices allowed greater awareness of the complexity and dynamic of my inner terrain, of essence, integrity and unity in my life. For me, the journal was a reminder of the legitimacy and wholeness of the inner life. This understanding was underscored by the "courage work" which I was doing with Parker Palmer. That work took its name from the example of Rosa Parks who in challenging segregation embodied the "courage to

∞

live a life divided no more." An inner-focused approach to leadership, teaching, and living, the "courage work" sanctioned stillness and reflection and acknowledged the relationship between the inner and the outer, between reflection and effective action in the world.

Within the "courage work," as well as in my other work with organizations, the structures from Ira's intensive journal process began to emerge as an aid for learning and leadership. Increasingly, in all my work, I provided participants with journals for reflection and built in time for them to use them. I began retreats, workshops and off-sites with a Steppingstones check-in: "What are the Steppingstones, choice points, events that have brought you to where you are in your work and your life?" I would ask folks to answer this question first in their notebook or journal, then to share some of their thinking with a partner, and finally to introduce themselves around the full circle by talking about what stood out for them when they did this exercise. At the suggestion of my colleague Diane Cory, I began to provide a bowl of small polished pebbles for folks to choose from to represent their Steppingstones. I opened most work meetings with a more subtle form of the steppingstone process: "Before we begin, let's take a moment to find out what brought each of us to this work." I also allowed people more time in silence to pull their thinking together and I usually framed work with a single powerful question rather than with a topic or a statement as I might have in times past.

Next I experimented with creating journals. Colleagues and I designed a learning journal for a network of corporate leaders working on employee engagement, and from that experience, those of us in the courage work designed a courage journal for our work with public school teachers. Out of that emerged a more generic journal, small simple, spiral bound, its pages sprinkled with block graphics and short pieces of poetry from many traditions, many cultures and many periods. I use it with almost

∞

all my work now, changing the cover to say "Notebook" in those cultures, like manufacturing, where the word "Journal" is too foreign. I remember one young engineer saying to me, "I turned the page to where this line of poetry is, and I found myself writing things I didn't know I knew. Strangest thing." The journal has spread to the work of colleagues, to college classrooms in distant states. I receive orders via fax from folks I've never met. One professor gave it as a gift to all his graduating seniors. The physical journal has become a way to reach out into the world in ways I alone can't. Like Ira, wordless, it gives permission to work on ones life, ones thinking, and I would now say, ones spirit.

I had not thought of the journal as spiritual discipline, for that's not a term natural to the mid-western farm girl in me. Rather I would have said it reconnected me with my own essence, values, perspectives, wisdom, truth. That it helped me see progress, to find my own path in the midst of complexity. Or that it helped me find in my life new energy, meaning, health, wholeness. Or that through its discipline, I was increasingly aware of and comfortable with awe, mystery, fear, love, uncertainty, complexity, paradox. And certainly it had opened me to my own creativity. But I didn't think about it in spiritual terms. I remember telling a colleague that I had no particular spiritual discipline. Startled, he responded, "Your poetry is your spiritual discipline." He was right and the poetry was the work of the journal.

I had also begun to experiment with journal media other than words, at times using acrylics, fine line magic markers, even newsprint and big magic markers, to represent thinking, feeling, to map inner terrain. My personal question about these alternative media was always "If I work this way, do I find fresh useful insights, do I feel healthier, am I able to move forward in my life, do I better serve the people and the causes I care about?" Julia Cameron's book *The Artist's Way* and Frederic Franck's process of "Zen drawing" were guides in my experiments with

∞

other-than-words in the journal. And those processes, too, found their way into my work with executives, as I experimented with shifts among words and pictures to alter perspective.

My story of the journal is not complete without touching on two other dimensions of inner work that link to it: music and the physical domain. It's probably no accident that as I returned to the journal, I also returned to the piano. While I'd played piano since I was five, regular disciplined playing ended about the time regular involvement with a spiritual community did, at the point of graduation from high school. But now, while working in the journal, I found myself writing about the influence of music on me. I began to use the video of the first Three Tenors concert as a way to explore shared leadership. I became familiar with the music of Michael Jones, his CD's, his book, *The Imaginative Life*, and the question that had taken him back to music: "If you don't play your own compositions, who in the universe will?" Recently someone asked Michael "How do you find your own music and how do you know it's yours." After a quiet moment he responded "Your music seeks you. It will find you in the stillness." The journal was the stillness in which my music could find me. It was one form of composition and actual music was another.

I noticed that being physically connected to music had special power for me. When Michael and I worked together I found any excuse I could to be near the piano. There I could feel the music. At home, I was playing the piano more and more for my own enjoyment, sight-reading pretty fluently again and accompanying the Sunday hymn singing before the start of Quaker meeting. One day, as a group of colleagues were working to design a seminar, Andy Bryner, author, recording artist, and expert in physical learning asked me if I played by ear and composed. I said "No. Never had. Couldn't. Never would." He asked me if I'd reconsider that belief, and with my permission, he removed all the music books from the piano, sat beside me in a rocker, and calmly coached me into playing without printed music. To my own

∞

amazement, I found myself playing my own compositions for almost an hour, without a "mistake." It was if the process of composing my life within the journal had suddenly arced like lightening from the journal page to the keyboard. The was a profound lesson for me of the untapped capacities we all have.

And at the same time, I began to explore physical ways to learn about the inner domain. My first learnings were with my Outward Bound colleague, David Starnes, with whom I partnered in work with executive teams. I could see how quickly folks "got" some of the ideas, without words. These initial experiences were followed with partnered work with the Center for Creative Leadership, and then with Dawna Markova and Andy Bryner in using the approaches of Aikido to explore paradox, subtle influence, deep listening. Our work incorporated "walk and talks," which are a structured inquiry with pairs of participants holding a focused dialogue on foot in a beautiful setting. All these explorations of the inner landscape resonated with what I'd learned with Ira.

In addition to the journal structures Ira designed, there are two other structures for use in the journal process that have emerged for me out of my own journal work, almost by accident. The first appeared one day when I found myself writing at the top of a blank journal page: "People who draw my best energies." I had no idea where that came from but it seemed worth exploring. I began jotting down the names that came to me of people who drew my best energies, in whose presence I was fully my best self. The list had no particular order. I wrote names at various angles here and there, until there were about twenty names on the page. Some were friends I no longer saw. One was a mentor, John Gardner, whose presence in my life had been particularly important during my years as a White House Fellow. Three were authors whose written work had given me hope and inspiration: Parker Palmer, Meg Wheatley and Peter Senge. The list had no visible pattern and no visible logic. I folded up the paper and put

∞

it in a pocket in my journal. Months later, something fell out of my journal and I picked it up, to find the list, which I had completely forgotten about. I looked it over with curiosity, and to my amazement realized that I was working with, or was in contact with everyone on that page. I had no idea how that had happened. My life was in a remarkably different place and I no longer felt stuck.

The second journal practice I developed, was to complete, every few months, a single journal page with this heading: "Things that I need as a regular part of my life to stay vital and healthy." On my list now go things like walks in nature, rich conversation, friendship, music, time with my children, healthy food, silence.

Despite the value of journal work in my own life there are some persistent questions that I continue to wrestle with in the journal practice both in my personal life and my work with organizations:

- To what extent is the structured Progoff journal unduly complicated and restricting with its different sections? Why the structure? Why not just regular notes or a diary? I think I am convinced that structures within a journal break us out of our thinking habits, and those breakthroughs move us forward in our life. And of course, there is no requirement to use all the structures all the time. One can pick and chose, realizing there still is synergy among the elements. Yet one could make a case for complete freedom as Julia Cameron does in her practice of morning pages.

- To what extent is it safe and appropriate for people to be known, open and so fully self-

∞

disclosing, in today's world or today's organization? A colleague from Arthur Andersen once asked me (when I gave the excuse of feeling vulnerable to prying eyes as the reason I had set aside the journal work years before), "And what do you think would have happened if they'd known who you were?" His question still rings in my ears today. In our lives, in our organizations, what do we think would happen if we really knew each other?

- To what extent does journal work record the "weather of the soul" and in doing so thus make the weather more "permanent" than it deserves to be? This is the question my meditation practice asks of my journal practice. I have come to the conclusion that for myself at least, recording our lives, good and bad weather alike, helps us understand life in a richer way, helps us understand how our own perspective on a single part of life can change. At the same time the journal helps us hold the threads of our lives more completely.

- To what extent does working with a journal and its structures bump up against dimensions of difference? What do we do about its unfamiliarity for many men? Is it an overly intellectual or verbal or literate medium that shuts out those for whom those channels are not the most fluent ones? How do we make journal structures natural, non-coercive, for a broad range of people? To what extent does working in other

∞

media like art, music and the physical arena, address these issues of difference?

- Is the whole idea, including structures like steppingstones and dialogue, just too darned personal or too soft for today's workplace? And if we "adjust" the structures to make them more business-like do we strip them of their power?

- And on the personal front, is journal work simply selfishly introspective and self-absorbed, and as such a reflection of a lack of commitment to important action in the outer world? Or is it a path to action of greater integrity and sustainability?

I believe these are important questions that one must live with if one adopts the discipline of a journal as a structure for inner work. But on balance, I find the journal, particularly the Progoff intensive journal, has had a healthy, centering impact on my life, my work and my spiritual life, broadly understood. The specific impacts, for me, include:

- greater ease with writing and self expression.

- a keener ear for my "inner teacher," my personal truth.

- stronger dialogue skills, including greater comfort with the process of spoken dialogue.

- the ability to get unstuck faster in the midst of difficult dynamics.

∞

- access to various forms of my own creativity.

- greater awareness of my gifts and my limitations, and increasing comfort with both.

- access to what I would call the logic of synchronicity, patterns more evident in journal pages than in the hurly burly of life.

- an ear for powerful questions.

- greater appreciation and love for human life in all its complexity.

- a new appreciation for the rich stories of others.

- the ability to be present to myself and others, more of the time.

- a more pervasive sense of peace.

- a greater sense of the simultaneous presence of mystery, awe, wonder, fun, joy, pain, fear and love.

- the capacity to move through rough emotional weather with greater honesty and grace.

- a trustworthy way to get back on path when I get off path, which is more often than I like to admit to myself or others.

∞

- a greater awareness of the power of my own experience. The capacity to as the Quakers say "Let your life speak," meaning, "Learn from your life. Listen to your own life, to its lessons for you, to its wisdom for you." The journal has helped me do that.

In closing: I have a particular place for journal writing—a corner of my glassed-in porch-office with candle lit in the pre-dawn hours. For years, I have sat thus, in beautiful space, in my mother's old white wicker chair, writing by candlelight before dawn, facing toward the center of the room, the woods behind me. Only recently when the clutter from a major redecorating project got to me did I change that ritual. One morning in desperation at the disorder in my line of sight, I picked up the old wicker chair, turned it around so I wasn't looking at the mess and sat down. Only to find myself facing a glorious sunrise through the oak trees, a view that had been there all along. That, I think, is a good metaphor for the journal itself: The journal process is about turning ourselves around and seeing a glorious view that was there, and all along.

∞

To Sit Simply

To sit
Simply
For one sweet hour
And notice
All that is
Unfolding
In the
Light of day—
That is
A fine, fine
Thing.

Life Dictates

"Life dictates much
Of what I do," I thought.
A role,
A should,
An ought,
A not,
A rule,
A discipline,
A job,
A necessary harshness,
Some kind of holding in
And holding on.

Then later on as
We all sat in silence,
I could see I had the
Kernel of a truth,
But had it wrong.

My life, as it turns out,
Does dictate much,
But not the way I meant.

It dictates poetry with
Truth so clear and solid
That it vibrates
Like a tuning fork,

And as it dictates thus,
Instead of closing ways,
It opens ways, it clears
A path I did not see.

Life dictates much,
Indeed, and doing so
It sets me free.

∞

The Ladder of Inference.

The ladder of inference is a way to map the processes of our own thinking, to make them conscious and then to share them with others as we move toward collective action. The foundational idea of the ladder of inference, from the work of the organizational learning community, is this: We take action as a result of meaning that we have created from inferences that we build like a set of steps up a ladder toward action—that's how it gets the name "ladder of inference." We tend to be unaware of the steps of our thinking. Awareness increases our ability to use the ladder to get better results. That's the ladder of inference, in a nutshell.

Now a deeper dive: There's not just one ladder. Each of us has one of our own with which we build meaning and take action in our own way. So imagine in your minds eye, that you have a big stepladder, with lots of steps, sitting in the middle of all possible data about the situation you are in.

1) The first step on the ladder, by which we make meaning so we can take action, is to select from all the data, the data that we consider relevant. So we don't look at all the data; we only choose the data that seem to us to be relevant. And from then on we only look at that data.

2) For me the next step is to put my feet on the step of feelings and emotions. What do those feelings do to begin to transform that data into some story that I can get a handle on?

3) And then we might step up a level in our thoughts about what's going on. What is the conceptual framework, the precedent, the logic that we bring to this, the thinking structures? So then we're on that step—of the thinking/ framework.

4) Then we step up another step: What assumptions are we making about how the world works, or should work, or what the other is up to? So we step up to the level of assumptions. We assume what the other is doing or thinking or wanting.

5) And then there is the step of our values. We step up to

∞

the way this situation impacts the values that we hold dear. What is at stake here that matters most to us? And we are on that step, now quite high off the ground of all data to consider.

6) And then we step up to what belief system do we hold as absolute, sacred, through which we reflect on where we now are in this situation? And how does the belief system shape what we see? And that's another step on the ladder.

7) Now we climb up to the next step: And what conclusion do we draw from all that, and that's the step of judgment, deciding. And that's a step high on the ladder.

8) And then the final step up, the furthest away from all the actual data: And then what action is therefore absolutely required? And from there we leap into action. And that's the top step on the ladder.

Now if you think of a regular step ladder, like one you'd have in your house—maybe a 6 foot step ladder, or even, if you have better equipment or do construction work, one of those big 12 foot step ladders. What does it say on the top step of a stepladder? It says: THIS IS NOT A STEP. DO NOT STAND HERE. That's what it says.

But it is from the top of that ladder that we take a stand. From the action that comes from the judgment, that comes from the beliefs that comes from the values, and the assumptions, that comes from the thinking, that comes from the feeling, that comes from the selective data. Like the old, old song "The ankle bone's connected to the leg bone, and the leg bone's connected to the knee bone, and the knee bone's connected to the thigh bone, now hear the word of the Lord...." And the result seems to us as

∞

incontrovertible as hearing the word of the Lord. But it's not the word of the Lord; it's just our particular ladder of inference. And to action! We dive in!

And we have some steps that we trust more than others. I trust my values as a solid step on which to move up toward action. I examine them thoroughly. But I am much less trusting of the data that I select, and I move through that step quite quickly. For those who know the Myers Briggs Type Indicator (MBTI) you might think of the intuiting, sensing, thinking and feeling dimensions as all steps on the ladder, and ones we trust more or less depending on our preferences.

Now you might say, "Well the steps of my ladder of inference include some other things." Fine, add those steps. And you might say, "And I don't include feelings, or assumptions, or some of the other things you've listed above." Perhaps. But remember that there are steps that are below the level of ones consciousness. We move so fast up that ladder, we are scrambling so fast with our minds that we move in a nanosecond from selected data to judgment and action. There may well be steps on our own ladder we don't know about.

There we are diving into action as if it is the only possible thing to be done—as if any decent human being, any principled person, anyone who cares, anyone who has half a brain, would obviously do the same thing.

So anybody who doesn't want to dive in now, this way, is obviously neither human, nor principled, nor smart nor caring. And all of that "knowing" happens with the speed of lightning. And we are zapped by the truth of our own knowing.

Now two things are going on, at least. 1) We move from all possible data to our conclusion and action in a nanosecond. Zap, and we are there. 2) And we assume that everybody else's ladder

∞

is like ours. They are moving the same way. Unless they are the enemy, or stupid, or wrong.

What does it matter that we are unaware of the ladder? After all we are unaware of the connections operating in our computers. We just see what's on the screen, not all the complexity that goes into what's on the screen. With the computer, we don't need to know. Why is our mind any different? With our minds, it would be helpful to be more aware, so we have a better idea of how we get where we get, and particularly if we don't like the results, how we might arrive at a different result. My variant on the wisdom of "If we do what we've done we will always get what we got." Is "If we think like we've thunk, we will always get what we've got."

But, you say to me, "I don't have time to think about this, or sort all this out within myself, let alone with others. I am already at my wits end with overload and demands and challenges." True. True. True. And it is awkward to begin thinking of such things. Awareness seems to get in our way, in the way of the efficiency, the elegance of action, the speed, which delights us as things now are. This is a big problem. Why would we want to do this?

And besides, we know from research, that it is the very ladder of inference that allows us to organize our experience sufficiently to be able to move about in this world. You may know of the research on folks who, blind from birth, are surgically given sight late in life. Without a ladder of inference, without having a lightning-fast way for organizing the swirl of dots and light and dark that they see, they are overwhelmed. In fact, some formerly blind people when faced with this swirl of stuff, prefer to put blinders over their eyes, because it is JUST TOO MUCH.

Sometimes I feel like that about trying to see all this complexity not in my usual way, but as discrete steps. IT IS JUST TOO MUCH. Too many data points. Too much confusion. Too much to consider. So I go back to my old way of thinking, just to get out

∞

of the difficulty of considering something else. And yet often there is pain and bad result in using my particular ladder, as I do. So I have a dilemma. When I become aware of my ladder, and start exploring its steps, I create an uncomfortable consciousness for myself, a kind of "loss of autopilot" and I may create a dilemma for you, if I ask you to examine your ladder as well so we can think better together. I have invited you into my dilemma, and into your own as well. Now we are both faced with an initially uncomfortable awareness.

The uncomfortable awareness reminds me of an old Peanuts cartoon: Lucy says to Charlie Brown, "Charlie Brown, I am aware of my tongue." Charlie asks, "Why would you want to be aware of your tongue?" "Can't help it. Just am." There's a pause and Charlie Brown says "Auggggg. Lucy, I think I am becoming aware of my tongue, too."

You may feel the same way about thinking about this. Augggg...now I'm aware of my thinking. And I don't see how that helps me. It's simpler to not be aware. How do we use awareness of thinking for better results? How do we move ourselves consciously up and down the ladder?

When we say things, when we tell ourselves the story of what is going on, we are moving ourselves up the ladder. Toward action. Away from data. There's nothing wrong with that at all. It is a necessary direction in life. But we may not have all the information in hand to jump into effective action. And we may be unaware that in addition to what we are saying out loud, to others, so they can track our thinking, we are also saying things to ourselves that we are not sharing with others. We may even be saying things to ourselves that are below the level of consciousness. (And that is what is known as the left-hand, right-hand column, in the community of organizational learning.)

∞

So the process of telling, of advocacy, of putting together a story moves us up the ladder. And if we want to work our way back down, we need to get back to the data, away from story. We need to ask questions.

Here is a process for consciously moving up and down the ladder, which I learned from my friend Dawna Markova, who, when I was most confused, conflicted, and struggling in my life, and wanted to jump to action and conclusion, would walk me up and down the street in front of my house, saying: "OK, now what do you see? And what is the story that you tell yourself? And what else do you see? And what do you tell yourself? And what else do you see? And what is the story you might tell yourself?" Then when I got the hang of walking with Dawna, and at her prompts, doing the exercise, I began to practice doing this alone, without her beside me: "OK what I see is this. And the story I tell myself is this. And what I see is this. And the story I tell myself is this. And what I see is this. And another story I might tell is this. Or I might tell myself this."

Realizing that we're never looking at all the data, only parts of it, I taught myself to say "And what I am not noticing, or not paying attention to? While I focus on this piece of data, here is this other piece of data.... And what story do I tell myself about that?"

And then I began to wonder, how do our ladders create our relationships? And the results of those relationships? This is a challenging question. And how do our ladders pop up unexpectedly when we least expect them, by throwing us into action prematurely?

Four or five years ago, my colleague Margie and I were part of a five day organizational learning program for Ford automotive engineers, and we were in charge of "teaching" the ladder of inference. Being hands-on folks, we decided to use a real stepladder with the steps marked appropriately on the ladder–

"data," "feelings," "logic," "values," "assumptions" –in order to demonstrate the idea of the ladder of inference. But in our concentration on our responsibilities for finding the perfect ladder (this one was a huge 18-foot yellow construction ladder that the conference center had in the shop) we lost focus on schedule. We mistakenly brought the ladder into the meeting room one day early—on Tuesday, rather than as scheduled on Wednesday, when our two male colleagues were expecting us to do that work. Our two colleagues, in the midst of presenting something else, looked at us stunned, when like some zany comedy routine, Margie and I came in the door struggling to carry this ill-timed and unexpected ladder. One of the guys looked at us in disbelief and said, "What is <u>that thing</u> doing in here today?"

It was a great moment. And it reminds me that when somebody's ladder of inference shows up unexpectedly or produces something very different than we expect, we often respond in that way. Where did that thing come from? What is that doing here, today? Why are they doing that? What are you doing?

Great questions. I thought we were doing OK and on schedule. What's the ladder doing in here, now? So what are the circumstances that send us for the ladder, running up the ladder? Lack of road signs about where we're going? Insufficient information? Not enough communication? Lack of guidance? A sudden sense of danger? A sudden change in direction? Silence? Unmet expectations? Fear? Confusion? What is it that sends us for the ladder and causes us to climb it, unthinking? What is it doing in here today? What if the need to examine the ladder is felt by one of us and not the others?

What is that ladder doing in here today and why have you dragged it in here? These are unspoken questions.

The work of the community, then, of those stewarding the commons, and what matters most between us, is to create a ladder

∞

we can maintain in common. And from which we can build the community we want. This is construction work of the most important kind. And as each of us becomes aware and respectful of our own ladders, we are more likely to be able to participate in that process of creating a ladder on the commons of our life.

∞

67
Trust equals speed

"Trust equals speed," he said
Explaining why we need
To trust at work. Trust
Lets us move ahead
With lightening speed.
I think he's right.

Yet trust takes time.
It's silent, too,
And meditative in its
Steps. It moves at
Paces that seem slow
And hesitating,
First one foot,
Then the next.

Trust is a dance
Developed over time,
A set of natural steps
Emerging from a bond
Forged from the passion
That we feel for dreams
We hold in common,
And respect
For all the ways we're not alike,
Both held, the dreams and difference,
Unflinching and aware,
Day after day,
As we work
Side by side.

Trust equals speed.
Yet it is utterly,
Completely still.
Trust is unmoving
And it is the speed
Of light.

∞

68
Things as they Are

To live with a full measure of real joy
Seems to require that we
Work with things as they now are,
And at the same time
Speak our hunger for our dreams,
For something well beyond
That which we see.
It means I feel the world
Imperfect, human, flawed,
Myself as well,
And know the vision
That I hold is present
In this moment that I live,
A treasure overshadowed
And not seen because
Not looked for, or not
Trusted, or just lost within
The dark and scary corners
Of the place where we now
Shine the light.
There is no other way to
Move toward joy, toward grace, vitality,
But to hold dreams
And loose them all at once,
To work with things as they emerge,
Seeing the tiny buds in need
Of time to grow, weeding the
Flat-leafed things that keep
The light from things we love;
Tending the little plants
Needing just light and space
And moisture to grow strong.
Despite my sense that action is
What life demands of me,
There isn't all that much I need to do
To make a space for what I love,
But to acknowledge that I love it.

∞

Cone in the Box or Why Airplanes Crash

About a decade ago I was working with a group of super-smart consultants who were in the midst of a strategic crisis. Although they were super-smart (by their own definition as well as the assessment of others) they had noticed that the reports they completed for clients tended to simply lie on the shelf and collect dust. And worse than that, the clients avoided return engagements with the consultants. When the consultants tried to find out why, they learned that in most cases the clients stayed away because of how they ended up feeling after the work: Something in the process which the super-smart consultants used to produce the reports left the clients feeling as if they were dumb. Being in the presence of someone who made you feel dumb was not pleasant, so the clients didn't voluntarily repeat the process. This was turning out to be a bad business development for the super-smart consultants.

The leadership of the super-smart consultants had come to the conclusion that the consultants needed better dialogue skills in order to communicate better with their clients. That, they thought would stem this tide of bad events. So they had sent the super-smart consultants to dialogue training to be fixed, and I was to fix them by teaching them dialogue. Of course, the leadership team wasn't in the room with the consultants and me. And thus I was standing before a group of skeptics, who didn't seem to be warming to the notion that a different quality of conversation might change their business fortunes.

I continued making a case for dialogue, for a different way of thinking about conversation, a different set of skills in addition to the analytical and debate skills that had brought them to such limited (and perhaps, limiting) success in their lives. In the midst of my expert and analytical case for dialogue, my colleague Bob

∞

Ginnett, jumped to his feet and said, "Let me show you why dialogue matters. And why airplanes crash."

He went to the board and sketched something that changed my life, and my way of thinking about conflict, forever: It was a three dimensional cone in a three dimensional closed box. He told us that while we could see the box, we were to imagine that the cone was completely hidden from our sight. The cone represented something very important to us and was key to our success. So we wanted very much to know what was in that closed box.

He asked us to imagine that the box had two tiny peepholes, one on the top of the box labeled "peephole A" looking down from above on the point of the cone, and another on the side of the box, labeled peephole B which looked in at the side of the cone.

What would someone at peephole A report seeing? "It's a circle." And those at peephole B? "It's a triangle." Which one is right? And how do we usually resolve such obvious differences in perspective?

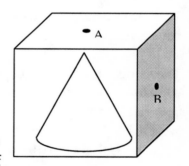

After a startled silence, the consultants began to explore what we need to do if something very important, and unknown to us can be brought into focus only if we share information that comes from two very different, and seemingly conflicting perspectives. What process do we use then? Debate or dialogue? Slowly, the skills of dialogue began to become more interesting to them.

I have continued this conversation about cone in the box for years now, with leadership teams across all sectors. I draw the box. And the cone. But I remind them they can't see the cone. It could be a giraffe for all they know. I ask the half of the room that represents peephole A, "What do you report seeing from your

∞

peephole?" "It's a circle," they will say. "And those of you at B?"
"It's a triangle." Later we will laugh about how quickly we move
from the question asking what we see to an answer of what it is.
The answer, "It's a...." of course doesn't answer the question as
asked. That shift from reporting ones perspective ("I see a....") to
announcing a fact ("It's a.....") happens in a nanosecond and we
don't even realize the shift we have made or how it gets us in
trouble.

"So, how do we usually resolve these different reports—It's a
circle, no it's a triangle?"

People laugh, and quickly respond, "If the person at A is the boss,
it's a circle." "Do we know what we have, by deferring to the
boss?" "No."

"How else do we resolve the difference?" With more laughter,
they say, "We debate and the best idea wins." Great. Now what
do we have? A winner. Do we know what is in the box? No.

"What if we vote?" What do we have? A majority. Possibly a
democracy. Do we know what's in the box? No.

"What if we all agree it's a circle, do we have a circle?" No, we
just have agreement. We still don't know what's in the box.

"What if everybody is at point A and nobody is at point B?" Does
that make it a circle? No. We still don't know what we have.

Sometimes we end up our conversation with this simple and quite
odd formula:
> If you win, we all lose.
> If I win, we all lose.
> If I win, I lose.
> A win-win is a win-win.
> A win-lose is a lose-lose.

∞

So what's called for is not a debate or a game where someone wins. What is needed is a process for placing individual perspectives on the table, side by side, and as a whole group taking them in. And we need to explore those perspectives, sitting until we are able to pull the disparate data into an understanding of what really IS in the box.

This may be the most profound and unshakable case for diversity and diverse thinking that can be made. If there is a perspective missing, we may not know what we are facing, and thus we may not have the data we need to avoid putting our lives at risk. Native American writer Paula Underwood reminds us of the stark reality of that danger in her book *Who Speaks for Wolf*. This is a teaching tale about one young member of the tribe who misses a critical decision-making meeting because he is out watching the wolves. And while he willingly agrees to support the tribe's decision (since he realizes he wasn't there when they were deciding) there is nonetheless a very dangerous outcome, which eventually weakens and threatens the tribe.

So in a period of about fifteen minutes, a simple sketch of a cone in a box changed my life. Pretty much permanently. *Cone in the Box* shifted my thinking about conflict (which I am adverse to). About difference (which I find difficult). About deference (which I am prone to). I realized that I could no longer hide behind the skirts of shyness, or deference, or politeness. If I really cared about the things that I said I cared about, I had to take consistent responsibility for reporting my perspective. And I had seen a picture that, for me and for many of the leaders I work with, makes it absolutely necessary to invite other perspectives, particularly those of people who have experience different from our own. Not because it is in style in leadership circles, and not because it is polite, and not because folks will then "buy into" the results (I HATE the term "buy in"). But simply because to not do so, means we don't know what is true, and puts everything we care about at risk.

∞

But back to why airplanes crash. That might still be on your mind. It surely was on mine, as Bob finished sketching the cone in the box. It turns out that he was an experienced pilot and had focused much of his academic research on cockpit teams, and how they make mistakes that result in crashes. What his research had uncovered, so he reported, was that almost anytime a plane crashed, the knowledge required to avert the crash was present "within the skin of the plane" but nobody paid attention. Now as a one-time flight attendant and someone who flies a lot for business, that caught my attention. Nobody was paying attention? Why?

It turns out there are lots of reasons, and all of them are relevant to leadership: sometimes folks were not paying attention because their focus was diverted to some unusual event, or they were watching an odd light on the instrument panel. Sometimes a junior flight officer saw something that seemed odd, but feeling junior, didn't report it, or reported it with uncertainty and it didn't get taken seriously.

Perhaps the most public and profoundly disturbing version of this dynamic would be the case Deborah Tannen cites in her book *Talking from 9 to 5*. She recounts the case of a co-pilot reporting ice on the wings who was ignored by the senior captain. The captain, as they rolled down the runway at take-off, whistled to cover up the co-pilot's words that "something is wrong here" before they dropped the airliner into the Potomac River. Seventy four people were on board. Only five survived.

But Ginnett reported that it wasn't always someone in the cockpit who saw something that was ignored. Sometimes it was the flight attendant who spotted something. Sometimes it was a passenger. What would they know, anyway? It's only a passenger.

For me the ultimate tale of a passenger being ignored (and this one ended happily) was the experience of an engineer who had

∞

helped design the supersonic Concorde. When the Concorde was being mothballed, the engineer decided he wanted to travel in it just once more for old time's sake. Sentimental reasons. Now picture this guy. Senior. Maybe tall. Probably imposing. Male. Settled back in his seat for one last flight from Paris to the US, in this technological wonder of the Concorde which he had helped design.

The Concorde had a history of blowing tires. It regularly blew tires on take-off . That seldom caused problems because of the redundant sets of tires. Still it was always a nagging concern. On rare occasions when the rim of a tire touched the runway, it threw off metal shards. That was considered more of a problem.

On the day our senior engineer was settling back in his seat as they rolled down the runway on take-off, he heard a tire blow and realized what it was, but of course wasn't troubled by it. However, seated by the wing window, as he was, he happened to be looking out as a metal shard thrown from the wheel pierced the wing and the fuel tank, and jet fuel began stream out. That, he knew was a BIG problem.

He hit the call button. The flight attendant came running, and he told her what he'd seen. "It happens all the time," she told him. "Sit down and buckle your seatbelt." Realizing the import of what he was seeing, he ignored her, unbuckled his seatbelt, and despite the fact that the plane was beginning to lift off the runway, he ran for the cockpit and begin pounding on the door.

The co-pilot came to the door, and over the words of the distressed engineer, ordered him to go sit down and buckle his seatbelt. The engineer, realizing his life and the life of everyone else on board was at stake, grabbed the co-pilot by his lapels, and dragged him down the aisle, and held his face against the window where he couldn't help but see the stream of jet fuel pouring out of the wing. When the co-pilot went limp at the sight, the

∞

engineer let go of him. The co-pilot ran for the cockpit, slammed the door behind him, and the Concorde immediately went into a tight turn back toward the airport where it landed safely.

Every time I think of this story it leaves me asking, "If a big strapping, experienced, senior male engineer, who helped design the plane, can't get heard, what hope is there for the rest of us–for the younger, slightly confused, uncertain people who might hold the critical piece of information that could save our lives?" And that leaves me always thinking of the stewardship responsibility we have as leaders to create the conditions for conversations that get critical perspectives voiced and listened to.

And at the same time, as an individual, whatever my role, I always have a responsibility to take my own perspective very seriously. Each of us may have critical information, perspective--- even if we appear to be seeing different things.

Of course, there are cases where what the other has to say is just plain wrong, untrue. Neils Bohr, explaining the nature of paradox, talked about the difference between simple truths and profound truths. A simple truth is clear and not so important: I say, "It is raining outside." Someone who says it is not raining is just wrong. Lying. The opposite of a simple truth, said Bohr, is a lie.

But there are truths of a different kind. Bohr called those "profound truths." So for instance, I might say that life is fragile. And you might say that life is resilient. And both are true. To understand life as it is, we need to hold both those truths at once. While it seems at first as if these are debatable points, debate misses the relationship entirely. Both are profoundly true. And like parents of twins, we have to hold both. This is the nature of a paradox.

∞

So when I clearly see a circle, and you, looking at the same thing from your perspective see a triangle, we are dealing with a paradoxical situation—one where two truths, two perspectives stand side by side. And to choose one over the other is to miss any chance to understand what we really are grappling with. Of course, there are also cases, where there are two or more points of view where whatever choice we make is fine as long as most of us go along with it. An obvious case would be something like "Where and when should we hold the holiday party?"

Meanwhile back at the cone in the box: "Now," you might say, "but why don't you just switch to each other's peepholes, so you see what the other person sees?" And with our notion of standing in the other's shoes, this seems at first like a good strategy. But our "peephole" is the result of our life experience, our entire way of seeing the world built over a lifetime, and so I can't switch to yours. Nor you to mine. You can't see the world as a woman of my generation from a small fishing village in the Midwest. Your experience has given you different perspective.

Or you might say, "Why don't we just take the box apart?" But the box that is limiting us is the box of our own way of thinking, of seeing. We can only see what we are seeing. And that box can only be "taken apart" or explored, by the quality of dialogue and inquiry that helps us see more and more of each others and our own thinking, that helps us understand more of the structures and experiences that have produced our perspectives.

So hope for our figuring out that there is a cone in the box lies in my asking you a quality of question that will draw out more and more about what you are seeing. And hoping you will do the same for me. And that by sitting together with what we are able to offer each other as a perspective we may figure out what could possibly be creating such divergent reports.

∞

Now beyond this challenging matter of the logic of perspective are findings from the science of perception. The biologist, Humberto Maturana helps us understand the science of perceptive processes. His findings suggest we must rely on each other's seeing, if we are to ever see the entirety of what is before us. And see it whole. Maturana's research suggests that when I see a tree outside my office here–that oak for instance, just coming into leaf–that at best only 20% of the picture I have is based on the current data that is coming in through my eyes. (That assumes my eyes are good and the light is good and I am really paying attention to the tree.) Eighty percent of the picture that I see in my head right now is based on my prior experience with that pattern of light and color, this time of day, this time of year, when I am sitting in this office chair, typing.

So we are, in an odd way, mostly captive of our experience. And yet at the same time, it is only our experience that gives us our ability to see. All we have to offer is our perspective. All we have to offer is the report on what we can see. Realizing all this makes me feel dizzy. And it puts me in mind of the odd research done on kittens years back to see how they learned to see. Some kittens just born were stitched on the back of other cats. So they didn't walk on their own. Each was just carried about on the back of another cat. No direct experience of walking. When the kittens' eyes opened, as they naturally do at a certain stage of development, the kittens on the back of another cat were blind. And for life. No feet on the ground early on, no sight? I like the metaphor. No experience? No seeing.

Yet Maturana would say, "Experienced? No way to see, solo. We need each other."

So if the *Cone in the Box* stands for matters of great importance to us, matters that are complex, and may well be dynamic, we need to be continually sharing reports of what we are seeing with each other. When what we are looking at and trying to understand is

∞

important, systemic and dynamic, then high quality conversation is essential and needs be never-ending.

Cone in the Box remains a simple way to remind us of our responsibility to offer the truth of our perspective, no matter how shy, deferential, junior or inexperienced we are. And no matter how experienced, expert and senior the other person is. It also reminds us that if we are the experienced one, we should be prepared, even anxious, to listen with an open mind and to be willing to shift our thinking as we hear the perspectives of others.

Cone in the Box also helps us remember the dangers of a system in which anyone, by pulling rank or exerting power, can silence others or any circumstance where one can use intellect to trump other forms of insight. Recalling cone in the box can make us naturally curious about what the other person is seeing. And finally, it encourages us to seek out processes and structures that make it natural, and easy, for those around us to offer their perspective, to report what they see from where they sit.

∞

Tad Mule

My friend Mary
Has hatched
A whole new
Word: "Tad mule"

It is a little
Notion
That grows up
To be
A stubborn idea.

I have those.

∞

Vast Sky

The sky here is
So vast it can
Hold opposites
Of weather at
One time—
Blue sky, a
Storm, a
Sunrise,
All at once.

If feelings are
The weather
Of the soul,
Perhaps
We're all
Montana skies,
Quite vast enough
To hold it all.

∞

Leading in Tough Times

Tough times are non-growth times, cutting times, times often too turbulent and uncertain for comfort. Such times reflect the continual turbulence and change that Peter Vaill talks about as "permanent white water" and the additional difficulties of a shrinking resource base. Many of us who enjoyed being leaders in the turbulence of growth times, when we had options and latitude, find the combination of constraints and unpredictability disheartening. But there is guidance available about how one leads in such tough times.

Some of that guidance comes from Vaill, in his book *Managing as a Performing Art*, reminding us that working harder, working politically smarter and working technologically smarter get us only part way to our goals. Particularly in tough times, we must, he suggests, turn to three other strategies: working collectively smarter, working reflectively smarter and working spiritually smarter. Working spiritually smarter, without reference to religion of any kind, means turning to core values for guidance.

Yet as leaders, our own instinct in tough times may be to turn away from others, to assume that as leaders we are being paid to make the tough decisions, to shoulder the inevitable burdens of leadership. That is sometimes true, but that mindset may lead us away from the human energies of others which would help us solve the problems. It leads us away from the option of working collectively smarter.

We may also insist that tough times mean aggressive fast response, and so we may deny ourselves the opportunity to be reflective. We lead ourselves away from the option of working reflectively smarter. And having denied ourselves the shared leadership dialogue of working collectively smarter, as well as the

∞

time to work reflectively smarter, we are no longer in touch with the values that would help us work spiritually smarter. So we are cut off from that leadership option as well.

Vaill also points us to the importance of recognizing and giving voice to the truth of the anguish of the organization and the pain in organizations during tough times. Gifted leaders acknowledge the anguish and help people move through it to superior performance. I recall one leader's start of a session on budget cuts. It was a classic in its recognition of anguish. Maryland's Secretary of Economic and Employment Development stood before his leadership group and admitted that he had not wanted to come to the session because cut-backs and scale-backs were the "pits." He talked of how "lousy" it felt to have these necessary and painful discussions. As he spoke honestly about the pain, the large "Maryland with Pride" banner, hanging behind him, peeled itself off the wall and fell on the floor face down. His folks roared with laughter. Both his words and the falling state banner were honest reflections of a difficult situation. Peter Senge in *The Fifth Discipline* calls this "honest talk about current reality," a kind of talk which he says is in woefully short supply in most organizations.

Compelling vision, honest talk about tough reality (hopefully with the leavening of some humor) and lots of information on the situation are requisite to good leadership. Also requisite is constant attention to issues of relationships. Meg Wheatley speaks of the leadership algorithm as an information rich environment, compelling vision and attention to relationships of integrity. Especially in tough times such factors are signs of effective leadership.

The trouble is that as leaders, tough times often push us to opposite strategies—we keep information to ourselves, we talk of survival tactics not vision and we get so busy that the relationships grow frayed. Like an inexperienced driver, coming

∞

into a curve, we hit the brakes instead of using the car's power to get us through the curve. The power lies in information, vision and relationships.

Down scaling is one of the reflections of tough times and it is undeniably tough for those for whom it means leaving the organization. But as difficult as down-scaling is for those let go, it is difficult in a different way for those who stay, those who survive. Whether those who survive the tough times are able to recommit, and to feel comfortable about what they have been part of, depends to a large extent on the way in which difficult decisions are handled, and the way that those who must leave the organization are treated. This is an important consideration, not only in treating well those who patently deserve it, but in treating in decent ways those who may not so clearly have deserved it. At issue here is a variant of the survivor's paradox. People are not able to recommit if the values they hold dear are decimated by the process, and if others have been treated unfairly and inhumanely—even if in the name of economically tough times. Economically tough times are the organizational equivalent of "the devil made me do it," an excuse transparent to all.

In a sense, tough times are the very time to put increasing energy and attention to values, to core beliefs, to the guideposts of humane leadership. We may have to make tough choices but we need to make them in a way consistent with our values, with the guidepost of true north in view. And if we find our values in conflict, values which must be balanced in new and uncomfortable ways, those new balances must be explored openly and directly with people.

We often find that threat and tough times cause self-managing teams—groups of people who over time have come to handle both task and relationship issues without much help from their leader—to become dependent again on their leadership for attention to both relationship and structure. Suddenly, leaders

∞

find they must build in time and emotional slack to address these unexpected demands. They must anticipate people hanging on their "door frame," beginning discussions which are pointless and unnecessary, seeking instruction on tasks already well understood. All this is the response of otherwise mature individuals, and otherwise mature groups, to the ambiguity of change and the fear of uncertainty. It is their way of checking the "trust" quotient, of seeing if the bonds, the relationships are still strong. But since most organizations don't sanction talk about feelings and bonds, the individuals talk about tasks, about "things." They talk of tasks, and things, but the real meaning of the discussion is all about trust, about bonds, about feelings. The wise leader understands this human need and is patient with people's need for his or her time.

While the process of handling tough times, of restructuring and cutting back, is rough and painful, it can be and must also be objective. If it is fair, and if the steps can be seen ahead, people can usually handle it. Our people are also more likely to weather the change if we can give them a longer view of what is happening, a clear sense of a positive goal (survival is not enough), and the capacity to put all this uncertainty in long-term perspective.

There is no simple recipe, no formula for handling tough times. It is not a matter of technique on the part of the leader. It is a matter of reaching deep into one's core for those inner resources which are sustaining when all else fails. Such resources are not tapped, nor built, by attention to the fine detail, and to the functional matters of the business (although all this is necessary) but rather to the broader issues, the broader values, and the broader view.

At an organizational level, we need to make sure that the fair processes and strong values necessary to weather tough times are in place long before the tough times hit. If they are not, trying to develop such processes and values in the midst of white water

∞

may result in a level of distrust and unwillingness to commit, that will render the process useless. We must ask ourselves if it is ever possible to build the culture while the boat is going through the rapids. I think the answer is "no." But these may be the times where many organizations must try this seemingly impossible task, and when some organizations learn the hard way that it is impossible to do so. The ability of the leader to be honest, direct, and open with the individuals in the organization—collectively, and in one-to-one discussion—is key to the healthy future of the organization. The wonderful frustration and frankness about budget-cutting being the "pits," as the "Maryland with Pride" banner peeled itself off the wall behind him, is a fine example of how a leader's honesty can open others up to speaking honestly, and enable them to get on with things.

Vaill points us toward an intense light, one from which we generally shield our eyes—the emotional and spiritual meaning of work and work communities, and the losses people experience there. Tough times intensify those losses.

Yet in tough times, the only really expandable resource an organization has is its people. The money is limited. The options are limited by tough external realities. The plant is fixed, and usually deteriorating. But the energies and spirit of the individuals in the enterprise remain surprisingly elastic—if there is a sense of trust, respect, and commitment by the leader to those served and to the values of the enterprise.

Of course, there are ethical dilemmas inherent in asking people to give more when times are tough—and when they can seemingly count less on the organization. But they can still count on each other. There are still webs of support and community in such organizations. Our goal should be to support those webs, and affirm them. And to realize that while there are fewer satisfactions in tough times, one of them remains the satisfaction of doing work well, of helping colleagues, of being competent, of

∞

being creative, of being heard. All these are no-cost items for leaders—and items which expand the human resource. So while the temptation is to cut back on people when times are tough, and to tighten up on people and to watch people and to cut costs, it may be important to send an alternative set of signals. Those signals should suggest that only in the creativity, persistence, productivity and passion of the individuals in the organization, is there an effective way through difficult times. Such a signal may tap the best energies of the organization.

IN SUMMARY, then I would suggest that in tough times, the organization needs:

- A goal more persuasive than survival—a positive beacon;
- A longer time horizon—a sense that this downturn won't last forever;
- A sense of history which enables people to see how the present compares with ten years ago—how these cycles have come and gone and the organization has survived;
- A sense of community—the ability to manage collectively smarter;
- An emphasis on core values like truth, trust, fairness, honesty—all of which seem to take more than the usual beating in tough times;
- A decision-making process fair enough so that those who remain feel good enough about the organization to recommit.

If these are the needs of the organization, then the leaders must:

- Repeatedly clarify the goal with language which is powerful, accurate, and compelling;
- Reframe the story to expand the time frames and provide perspective on the current difficulties;

∞

- Tap the collective wisdom. Many heads are better than one;
- Keep focused on the core values of the organization and reflect them in every way possible;
- Provide enough time in the leader's own schedule to stay in touch with the human side and touch base with fundamental values;
- Pay attention to both task and relationship issues in the organization;
- Be willing to acknowledge the anguish.

These are the requirements of leading in tough times. Like a driver coming fast into a curve, we must resist our temptation to hit the brakes, but rather keep our foot steady on the accelerator, a steady attention to the human side, the values side and the deep meaning that work and the workplace has for each of us.

∞

Because you have no money

Because you have no money
Don't believe
That you must squander
What you have
In such abundance:
Time together,
Joy,
Attention,
Challenge,
Your good work.

∞

Cynicism in the Workplace

Cynicism
In the workplace,
Like anger
When a love affair goes sour,
Is about passion disappointed,
About heartache,
About grief.

Dreams dashed
And promises denied
Harden the heart
That planned to offer
Everything,
And now has come
To offer but a wary wondering
And tiny bits
Of reserve energy
Carefully meted
Out.

∞

Trough

There is a trough in waves,
A low spot
Where horizon disappears
And only sky
And water
Are our company.
And there we lose our way
Unless
We rest, knowing the wave will bring us
To its crest again.
There we may drown
If we let fear
Hold us within its grip and shake us
Side to side,
And leave us flailing, torn, disoriented.

But if we rest there
In the trough,
Are silent,
Being with
The low part of the wave,
Keeping
Our energy and
Noticing the shape of things,
The flow,
Then time alone
Will bring us to another
Place
Where we can see
Horizon, see the land again,
Regain our sense
Of where
We are,
And where we need to swim.

∞

Living, Leading and Working
with Natural Human Fears

I expect we all have our anxious moments. Something scares us to death, knocks us off center. Startles us. Maybe it's a snake. Or a mouse. Or an unwelcome surprise. Something comes at us out of left field. Who knows what. For me it's wasps and hornets. At such times, we usually know we are scared.

Or it is more serious: The death of a friend. A car accident. A close call of some kind. We end up shaken. For a while. Perhaps for a long while. There is no question that we are scared, afraid, anxious. And we know the reason why.

But lots of other times, our anxieties and worries lurk beneath the surface. They are hidden even to us, papered over by our own sense that courage and bravery, and being a good mature adult, require putting on a brave face and not being afraid.

Parker Palmer suggests to us, in his work on the inner dimensions of leadership, that fear is natural to the human species and is to be expected. To have moments of fear is to realize that we are human, that all humans have things that scare them. It is as natural to have our fears as it is to have a wrist, or fingers, or a ribcage. It comes with the territory. Visible or not.

And what is true about the naturalness of human fears within us (whether we are aware of them or not) is equally true of all those around us. Those with whom we live and work. Those strangers we pass on the street. Each and every one wrestles, consciously or not, with fears. And the challenge for us all is to acknowledge the truth of our fears, and not let them run the show.

Daniel Goleman, in his work on emotional intelligence, provides a scientific view of where those fears have come from: We evolved

∞

in the cave and the savannah, where when something came out of left field and surprised us, it was likely to be a saber-toothed tiger. In that earlier world where surprises were indeed life-threatening, the question our inner-life-saving-self asks when startled is always is "Do I eat it or does it eat me?"

Unfortunately, now, in contemporary times, when the surprise out of left field is our boss asking us where the report is that was due Thursday, our inner "reptilian self" still asks the age-old question that comes from the age-old fear—"Do I kill him or does he kill me?" And in some of the greatest conflicts in which we participate, those ranging from personal disagreements, to local political squabbles, to neighborhood outrage at a development going up, to divisions across a nation, to wars among nation states—in each of these, the old primordial sense that our life is at stake, moves our gut out way ahead of our head. Robert Bly, the Minnesota poet, in his poem entitled *"One Source of Bad Information"* captures the way the inner voice gives us advice that once (thousands of years ago) saved our lives but makes little sense today:

> There's a boy in you about three
> Years old who hasn't learned a thing for thirty
> Thousand years. Sometimes it's a girl.
> This child had to make up its mind
> How to save you from death. He said things like:
> "Stay home. Avoid elevators. Eat only elk."
> You live with this child, but you don't know it.
> You're in the office, yes, but live with this boy
> At night. He's uninformed, but he does want
>
> To save your life. And he has. Because of this boy
> You survived a lot. He's got six big ideas.
> Five don't work. Right now he's repeating them to you.

Yet we have a choice: Will we "be fearful"—that is will we <u>be</u> our fears, live from our fears, be a manifestation of fear? Or will we

∞

live from the paradoxical power of compassion, respect, curiosity, love, faith, and abundance? (Remember that the definition of paradox is two seemingly contradictory fundamental truths standing in relationship with each other.) Of course most all of us think we would choose the more enlivening state of living from those other values. But do we?

It is challenging to realize that to live with paradox doesn't mean ignoring fears at all, but rather accepting them compassionately as a part of our human make-up. And realizing that they have an old, perhaps limited, but still valuable, wisdom. They have "saved our life." There are indeed things that really can be dangerous in our world.

And to sort out whether the thing that feels like a saber-toothed tiger in our life really is dangerous, or simply one of Bly's five ideas that don't work any more—that sorting out takes time, and increasing levels of self awareness. It means getting increasingly familiar with our inner terrain—the beauties of that inner terrain as well as its swamps, the parts of the terrain, like swamps, that are less pleasant and harder to explore. (A friend of mine said, "Would it help if you called it a "wetland" and not a swamp?")

All of us need to do that work of exploring the inner swamps, so that we aren't living in ignorance of what's going on with us. But those who are leaders of any kind, whether by position, title, or simply by longing to take action in the world, from wherever they sit—those who are leaders have an additional reason to get to know that terrain, and to be aware of the role of natural human fears in their lives. Because the leader's impact on others is so great, their unconscious fears can create a world of fear around them and can multiply the very fears they wish to submerge.

And that's where the matter of fears common to all of us, and leadership come together.

∞

If I am serious in caring about what I care about, what leads me to aspire to, and act on, leadership instincts within myself, then I must be serious about exploring the inner terrain that shapes my outer actions. Stern words, but warranted. As they say in the South, "Listen up."

The simple grid that follows builds on Parker Palmer's notions of the five natural human fears, taken from his original essay *Leading from Within*, now a part of his book *Let Your Life Speak*. The left-hand list is the fears. The right hand list sketches the countervailing facts or belief states that stand as a paradoxical truth with those fears.

The middle column represents the "shadow" cast by leaders on others around them (how others feel they are being treated) when the leader is unable to admit to consciousness the natural human fears that she experiences. It's an odd and perverse kind of "hydraulics": when a leader pushes his or her natural human fears out of awareness, she instead unknowingly projects them onto others, unwittingly creating an organizational culture of fear and lifelessness at the same time insisting on her own fearlessness.

One can think of the third column as "countervailing facts" or "thinking structures" or "faith statements." Nevertheless, one ends up in the same place no matter what phrase you choose. It's the inner awareness that is critical.

∞

Fears (natural to all human beings)	My fears, when ignored, cause me to treat you and others as if . . . (projections of my fears onto you)	Countervailing facts that balance fears
1. I'm not enough; I don't have what it takes.	1. You're incompetent.	1. We have birthright gifts yet untapped and learning capacities untouched.
2. It's a tough, cruel world out there. Life is a struggle.	2. You're attacking me, competing with me, out to get me.	2. Despite examples of scarcity and brutality, there is much abundance and generosity in the world. The world is often a place of awe and wonder.
3. I can only count on myself. I must do it alone and I'm in it alone.	3. Your offers of help are not to be trusted.	3. Help and connection with others are everywhere around us, although sometimes in places and forms that surprise us.
4. The chaos is taking over. I am losing control.	4. Your meddling, creativity, ideas and involvement are contributing to the chaos, the loss of control.	4. In ambiguity and seeming chaos, lie surprising possibilities and great creativity.
5. I won't be able to handle the losses that are ahead of me.	5. You are afraid of change and I must subtly coerce and manipulate you into my plan for the future.	5. From loss, even from death itself, comes renewal and new life.

Appreciation to Parker Palmer for his notion of the five fears in *Let Your Life Speak*.

∞

Connection

It is
A massive place
And old,
Built for
Another time
And place,
Yet working still.

A place where people
Work the presses,
Handle steel,
Make coils of rods,
Shape car parts,
Pass them on,
One to the next.

If you want
To be heard
Above the din,
You have to touch
Each other,
Standing very close,
Leaning into words near lost
Within the vastness
Of the place.

One man,
Explaining what he did,
With pride,
Touched me
To draw me near
So I could hear.

Touched me,
This stranger did.
I heard his
Every word.

∞

Learning from Strangers;
Leadership Lessons for a World of Diversity

Why does tapping the talent of diverse cultures matter? All the obvious reasons, like the world is more diverse and if we don't get this right we will blow the place up. And the country is more diverse and if we don't get this right we will blow it up. Or the business will fail. Or I will fail. Actually these reasons, while they get my attention and stop me in my tracks, aren't very motivational. They don't move me.

What moves me are more nuanced, positive and personal reasons: the sheer joy of reaching across boundaries of difference and being met. The richness of having the wisdom and knowledge that we can't possibly have within ourselves offered to us by someone different from us. The excitement of being a stranger in a strange land with the sheer terror and openness that we experience. It is why we are drawn to exploration and journey. Those reasons. The reasons that bring us alive.

Who needs to think about this? I do. We all do. None of us is immune from our own blind-spots about other cultures, other frames of reference, the value that other experience could offer us if only we could take it in, the way we wall ourselves from diversity of one kind or another. There are certain points of view or practices that seem so silly to me, or so unacceptable, that I walk away from them, unable to take them in constructively. Unable to learn from them, and unable to learn from my reaction to them. Unable to hear, unable to listen.

And there are behaviors of others, toward me, that silence me and dampen my participation. Each time that happens, I have to decide whether or not to speak my truth, and risk being marginalized for being "silly" or "thin-skinned" or "unsophisticated" in the eyes of others, particularly those whom I

∞

respect and care about. Current case in point: With several women colleagues, many fairly prominent in leadership literature, I am aware that several of our close and prominent male colleagues, of whom we are very fond, and who are themselves major figures in leadership theory and practice, are in the process of creating a global organization which they have given a name the resulting acronym of which is GIRL. Gently at first, and then less gently, women whom they know well have said to them that the name will eventually be reduced to the acronym and that the result is offensive to many women. As the acronym BOY would be for African American men. Fairly simple idea. While the intent is innocent, the likely result over time is, and will be, offensive to many. So far, the advice has fallen on deaf ears. These are bright, talented, and decent people. Yet they cannot hear what we are saying.

I realize I had to take a deep breath before even telling this story, out of my own fear that the reader will think me silly and marginalize me. Who would take seriously the writing of someone so thin-skinned? And that worry leaves me asking this: How many paragraphs like this go unwritten, held in the minds of those who see the world differently than I do? How many letters like those of Martin Luther King go unsent out of fear that they will be received with derision? How many Rosa Parks continue standing at the back of the bus? How can we, as leaders and educators, invite and welcome a different response from each of them?

None of us is immune from our own blind spots. We need each other to become aware of them. And once aware, we need the information then available to us from that unexpected quarter, in order to together, create the world we want.

∞

What does the field of leadership have to say about leading in diverse cultures?

If you frame the field in a narrow way, with the usual leadership literature, there is not a lot of mainstream leadership literature that is explicit about it. Having said that, I take guidance from the words of John Gardner, in various of his books, about the leadership potential within each of us. And I take guidance from his action: the creation and design of institutions (the White House Fellows, Common Cause, the Urban Coalition, the Independent Sector) all meant to elicit and solicit the broader range of leadership.

I take guidance from books that point to the natural world as a guide, in its natural abundance and healthy diversity, suggesting a world of healthier organizational life. The work of Peter Vaill encourages us to work reflectively, collectively and spiritually smarter—rather than trying to work individually harder and technologically harder. And collectively means all of us, together.

I pay attention to Ron Heifetz' work on helping organizations and societies learn their way through territory in which neither the nature of the problem nor the nature of the solution are within their experience base. In that world, the more diverse the bases of knowledge the safer we all are. And I take guidance from the work of Parker Palmer whose guidance in *Let your Life Speak*, about being present to the stranger across from us, and getting to know the shy stranger within us, stays with me daily.

At a recent conference that I attended, one of the participants, introduced himself and spoke of the guidance he took from Parker's work: "I'm ... a queer dad with two toddlers in a remarkably tension-free blended family. A practicing poet. A big bellied talker...my father self-identified as a medium and my mother as a Smith girl....Last fall someone gave me a copy of Parker Palmer's *Let Your Life Speak* and aside from being

∞

surprised about how much I was learning from the wisdom of a straight, white man, I suddenly realized I perhaps wasn't as crazy and alone as I thought."

Why might there be so little in the mainstream leadership literature?

Perhaps the lack of theory is because in other cultures, guidance about leading and shaping the world isn't written as theory-based social science literature. It comes to us as folk-tale, or poetry, or oral tradition like that reflected in Paula Underwood's *The Walking People*. And perhaps the silence in leadership literature is because the work about the dynamics of power and exclusion/inclusion has been more fully developed in the fields of sociology and psychology, than in the field of leadership, or even of the related field of political theory.

What invites the voice of the other, the stranger?

Now and then, I notice with surprise and curiosity those circumstances where what someone does as a leader or educator seems to draw out, or strengthen, voices usually silent. These are instances where those from the non-dominant culture suddenly are enlivened, engaged, participating, wading in with confidence. These are times when I can see visible engagement of people who often are not drawn to speaking out or otherwise exercising explicit leadership.

Since I spend most of my work-life working with organizations as a thinking partner, coach and leadership educator to organizational leaders of one kind or another, much of my own learning about what seems to elicit engagement in diverse cultures, goes on in workplaces of all kinds: symphonies, non-profits, big urban libraries, manufacturing plants, universities, government agencies. Now and then I am surprised by the sudden active participation of non-US-natives, people of color,

∞

younger staff members. One particular experience stands out for me and holds some notions of what makes a difference in tapping the energies of those often silent:

I was part of a working group helping a manufacturing client partner design an off-site for the leadership from the fifty-two manufacturing plants worldwide for which he was responsible for quality. He was worried that the plants' bad parts per million (PPM's) were at a level higher than the single figure target that he had set, and that he believed was essential to the firm's competitiveness as well as to their cost targets. Things weren't looking so good.

He was frustrated that he couldn't get the leadership of those plants to understand the importance of a "cadence," of an essential "rhythm" to manufacturing, a pace, and a meter that creates conditions for a higher level of quality. "They just don't seem to get the cadence," he said, slapping out a cadence on the top of the conference table to make his point. "And if they even get it, they lose it and can't get it back."

Without censoring my thinking, I looked at him and said, "Jazz band." "Hire one," he said. So we hired a jazz band for the off-site. We rehearsed with the band and coached them to play well, and then (much to their dismay) to begin to "lose it," that is to nose into what they called a "train wreck" and then to pull out of it.

A group of quite fine university musicians, they found it hard to believe that we wanted them to play badly when they could play so well, but they were willing to give it a try.

The next day at the off-site, the jazz band was to be the surprise. 250 manufacturing leaders from around the world had sat at round tables through the morning sessions of stats on quality, and had listened with interest, and probably some skepticism, to some

∞

examples of things going well in some of the plants and how the leaders had gotten those good results.

Then the surprise: Welcoming the band onstage, our leader invited everyone to now take a lesson from jazz, and listen to the musicians to see what we could learn about the process of shared leadership. What did we see about passing the leadership and what did we see when the band began to "lose it"? He asked us to notice what happened when the musicians found themselves moving toward what jazz musicians call a "train wreck." A "train wreck" was a fairly graphic term for what was happening in some of the plants. But the plants often couldn't pull out of the train wreck, like the jazz band could. And the question for all of us was, how did the band do it?

They began to play. We listened and watched them. They played well, and then slowly went into a "train wreck," beginning to lose the cadence and the thread of the theme. Then pulled themselves back on track. We asked them to do it again, and again all of us listened.

Then we had a conversation. All 250 of us. I asked how many folks played an instrument themselves. Many hands went up. I was surprised. It was an engineering crowd, and I wouldn't have expected so many musicians. "And how many of you have family members or close friends who are serious musicians?" More hands than before. Interesting. " How many of you enjoy music?" Almost all the hands went up.

"So what did you see when the band played?" All over the room, hands began going up: "I heard the way the theme got set, and then passed from one person to another." "I could see how the leader could step back and the process just did its own work." "I heard how the cadence stayed the same." "I got to thinking about how much they must have practiced individually to get this good." "And they must have practiced together a lot too." "I

∞

could see how much fun they were having." "It looked like such fun." "It looked so easy when it was working."

"And what about the train wreck? What did you see there?" "Well, at first I couldn't even hear when they were getting off-track, but I could see them looking toward each other for the first time, like they were checking on something." "Yeah, when they started to lose it, they turned toward each other and seemed to be watching and listening to one another more than before." "Yeah, when it was going fine, they were more off in their own world, but as soon as something wasn't quite right, they turned toward each other and moved closer together." "And they seemed to turn toward the band leader for him to set the pace." "Yeah, but they were each working on it." "They didn't give up at all. They just seemed to assume they could all get it back together." "You know, I never could spot when they were getting off track: they were so good they just got back on before I could hear anything." "Well, I'm a pretty serious musician, and I could hear it happen from the very beginning. So maybe it takes some practice to spot it early." "Maybe some folks can spot it before others." "And maybe we need them to."

"And when you head into a train wreck in a plant, what do you do?" Laughter everywhere. "We hunker down and blame the other guy." "We pretend it's not happening at all." "We avoid looking at one another." "We stare at our shoes during the operating committee meeting." "We blame the union." "The union blames us." "We say, 'Well there are places doing a lot worse than us.'" More laughter.

It was such a lively conversation, and so natural, that only about fifteen minutes into it did I notice something very unusual about what was going on. In a group where the conversation would usually be led by and dominated by the comments of the higher-ups, the manufacturing "gray beards," and the Dearborn based engineering powers, suddenly without my having noticed it, the participation was coming instead from the younger engineers, the non-native English speakers, people of color, people from outside the US. The leadership and the insights were being offered by cultures other than ours. We had crossed into a multi-cultural world without realizing it, and in that minute, I knew I wanted to find out how that happened.

What leadership or educational approaches create conditions that thus engage a multi-cultural world?

That question began to draw my curiosity. So I began watching everywhere for clues. In my own work as a leader and educator. In the work of others. From that experience base, I began to see these leadership principles that seemed associated with that higher level of engagement across dimensions of difference. Here are my candidates for what makes a difference:

Full bandwidth. Whatever we do that allows us to tap more diverse parts of ourselves and others, also allows us to offer many doors to connecting with the other. What stretches our bandwidth, invites others of a different bandwidth.

Listening as if our life depends on it. Whatever we do that allows the other to experience our genuine interest in and curiosity about experience and wisdom beyond, our own, engages others, particularly others visibly different from ourselves. It invites them to operate more actively in the enterprise, and eventually in the leadership of that enterprise. The key is listening as if our life depended on it, which of course, it does.

Awareness. Reality based awareness, or as a wise colleague calls it, "bare awareness." Being willing to perceive things as they are, without needing to analyze, or understand, or know what to do about it.

∞

Wide welcome for wisdom from unlikely places.
Listening for wisdom everywhere. Without judgment of where it
is to be expected. (Remember "Cone in the Box.")

**Wide latitude in our thinking about what counts as
leadership.** By talking about leadership as a capacity in all of us,
not only those at the top, or in one line of training or work, or who
only operate in one way, we open the field to many who don't
have a long heritage, or extensive personal experience in
traditional leadership.

**Big open softball questions and curiosity about the
responses to them.** Whenever we practice genuine listening and
learning across boundaries of difference, strangeness,
disagreement and/or conflict, we increase the probability of a
richer, better outcome. This means living from the point of
questions rather than answers, from the place of wondering rather
than certainty.

**Some concluding thoughts about how leaders can create those
conditions.**

Whatever we do that allows us to tap more diverse parts of
ourselves, also allows us to offer many doors to connect with the
other. What stretches our own band-width, invites others of a
different band-width.

Whatever we do that allows the other to experience our genuine
interest in and curiosity about their experience and wisdom, also
engages them more actively in the enterprise. And eventually that
practice invites them into the leadership of that enterprise as well.

Whenever we conceptualize leadership in our own heads, and
out-loud to others, and make clear that it is a domain of those
everywhere in the enterprise and note that leadership can be

∞

practiced in myriad ways, we open the space of leadership to many who otherwise would consider it closed to them.

And as we pursue these broader richer forms of leadership, and invite others into that space by practicing disciplined listening and learning across boundaries of difference, strangeness, disagreement and conflict, we increase the probability of a richer, better outcome, and of a dispersed leadership well beyond the usual narrow boundary of sameness that plagues us and places us and our organizations at risk.

Everybody Counts

Everybody counts.
When the spider
Weaves the web
No connecting point
Is missed.
If you are missing
From our midst
We are the lesser
For that loss,
And incomplete.

∞

The Rule of Six

One night at a party, a group of us began talking about "The Rule of Six," a Native American thought-pattern that I have found useful in my work with organizations, as well as in my personal life.

Others around the table had also found the idea very useful in work situations, and asked if there was something written down on it. I said I didn't know of anything, although undoubtedly the Native wise woman, Paula Underwood (author of *Who Speaks for Wolf* and *The Walking People*) who taught it to me, has written of it somewhere in her work. Years back Paula had provided a seminar for corporate leaders and consultants to help us understand what the Native American tradition might teach us "corporate types" about the nature of change. One of the most powerful lessons was "The Rule of Six." So I promised to put down on paper my (mid-Western, non-Native) understanding of "The Rule of Six" for whatever use folks could make of it.

How does The Rule of Six work?

When we are trying to figure out something perplexing (for which we often use the term "a problem"), or when we are facing into uncertainty, (for which we use the term "change") it seems natural to our western way of thinking to quickly try to find the right answer to questions like this: "Exactly what is the cause of this? What's going on here? How are things going to unfold? What is likely to happen? What should be our plan?"

Many of the most heated arguments, whether within our own heads, or among colleagues or with family members, are about who has the one right answer to those question before us.

∞

The "Rule of Six," a Native American thinking process or discipline, requires that instead of coming up with one single answer to the question, (which comes, of course from the story we tell ourselves about what is going on) we instead come up with at least six possible, or good, stories about what is going on. And then having done that, we hold all six stories in our head, and do not choose among them.

This is very hard for the Western mind. Even when we think of two possibilities, it is for the implicit purpose of having those two possibilities fight it out, until one wins. Thinking about more than one cause of an event or more than one possibility of an outcome is, in our mind, simply an invitation for us to quickly choose the right one. In fact, we move so quickly from what we observe, to the story we tell ourselves about that observation, to a conclusion, that we hardly realize that there is a space between what we see and the story we tell ourselves about it. We go from perception, to story, to conclusion in a nanosecond. We collapse awareness into action as if they were a single thing.

The Native tradition, by contrast, holds that there is a generous and open space after we notice something. And that is the space within which to hold many possible interpretations, or causes, or developments.

The ability to hold six possibilities in our mind accomplishes several things. It keeps our perceptions open to a wider range of data; it allows us to be "systems thinkers" seeking multiple roots of causality in multiple dimensions of a situation; it keeps folks from having to fight with each other about who is right at a time when they should be listening with curiosity to why each other sees things differently. And since we are not forcing ourselves to invest our ego in a single "best" idea, we naturally become more flexible in our thinking, and if our "favorite" of the possibilities doesn't turn out to be born out by the unfolding of data, we can more easily shift our emotional commitment to another idea

∞

which in the course of time has proved stronger. And we can make that shift earlier and more easily. So in a sense, the Rule of Six allows us to make necessary decisions, yet remain aware and realistic, more flexible in our thinking, present to the world and to the thoughts and perceptions of others, and perhaps even more compassionate with ourselves when we are "of two minds" or more, about something.

A personal discipline to increase "rule of six" capacity

My friend Dawna Markova (author of *No Enemies Within* and *I Will not Die an Unlived Life*) has taught me a walking meditation that I use when I am struggling with something, which can serve as a companion to "The Rule of Six." It goes like this. You walk, alone or with a friend, and say, "What I notice is this...." "And the story I tell myself out it is that...." "What I am feeling is this...." "And the story I tell myself is that...." What I hear is this...." "And the story I tell myself is that...." (On the one hand, and on the other hand. On the one foot, literally, and on the other foot.)

Having worked on the mental discipline of observation, story, observation, story, you can begin to work on the discipline of multiple stories: "What I notice is...." "And the story I tell myself is...." "Another story I could tell myself is ....and yet another story I could tell myself is...And a fourth possible story is...."

This meditative discipline enlarges the space between the perception and the story, or judgment, or decision. And it increases our ability to see many possible stories, and hold them all, in the same way "The Rule of Six" does.

A link between the Rule of Six and Scenario Planning

This year in a course I was teaching on the leadership of non-profits, we began to see the way in which the Rule of Six was like "scenario planning" the process made popular in the book *The Art of the Long View* by Peter Schwartz. Scenario planning requires the

∞

mental discipline of going out in time (five or ten years) and looking back to the present moment, then telling five or more stories of how events unfolded in vastly different ways, for a community, or an organization. (It was Royal Dutch Shell which first used this thinking discipline to "prepare" itself for the surprise of the 1973 Oil Embargo). One is required to name the various stories that unfold, and to make sure that one is an "unspeakably awful" alternative, and one is the current "favorite" and that a range of other possibilities are developed in great detail. Having developed those stories about the unfolding of events from a present moment toward a future yet unknown, one has then accomplished several important shifts in mind-set:

--One has spoken the unspeakable, and therefore lessened the grip of unspoken fears about the seemingly awful alternative;

--One has found ones own place, or role, within a range of possible futures; and one can see that all are survivable, or even have unexpected plusses;

--One has identified certain key "events" or "surprises" that would indicate that one or another scenario is unfolding, and one has lived that scenario fully enough in ones mind to be able to step quickly into the surprise (that is the Royal Dutch Shell story);

--One can see that there are certain "no-brainer" actions that need be taken immediately under any scenario, and one is energized to do those things. This breaks the usual trance which uncertainty engenders: Often the uncertainty about the future keeps folks frozen waiting for the clarity they believe they need in order to act. But no matter how great the uncertainty, how dire the straits, there are usually certain good things to do, no matter what. As a friend of mine in Detroit often says, "I can't know who will head the company tomorrow, but whoever it turns out to be, it will have been a good thing, today, to have made perfect quality car parts and shipped them to the customer on time."

∞

The natural world reminds us of the Rule of Six

I have found that it is one thing to know intellectually about the Rule of Six, and another thing to be able to live it naturally, when we feel pressure. Still there are reminders of the wisdom of the rule of six everywhere in the natural world. When I was recently on an Outward Bound canoeing expedition, I caught myself wanting to figure out in advance the "right way" to get down the river. Day after day I learned there were always multiple paths down the river, and the better of the ways only became evident as we were in the canoe on the river.

If you have done any farming, you know that when the crops fail, or you have bumper yields, there are always multiple reasons: weather, soil quality, soil preparation, pests, seed quality, timeliness of harvest.

The best natural reminder of the Rule of Six came to me recently, with perfect serendipity. I was working with colleagues who head a retail business, and we were sitting at the picnic table in front of my house, on a sunny day, talking about the rule of six, and how it might inform the strategy for their 25-year old enterprise. The neighbor's cat sprang up on the table and began walking all over our papers, nuzzling folks for attention, purring. Up and down the picnic table, pacing back and forth, purring. I kept pushing her out of the way. Finally a colleague asked me the cat's name. I pointed to her funny paws, with the six fingers, "Six," I said, pushing her aside, yet one more time. "The cat's name is Six." We burst out laughing.

So now, I am trying to keep my eyes open to the many ways the natural world provides us with evidence of the power of the rule of six.

∞

I welcome your thoughts about these ideas, and any experience you have using them.

PS. I faxed this note to Paula Underwood, and she liked it and sent me in exchange, a left brain and right brain versions of the rule of six.

The Rule of Six: For the Left Side of the Brain (written by Paula Underwood)

For each apparent phenomenon, devise at least six plausible explanations, each one of which *indeed* explains the phenomenon. There are probably sixty, but if you devise six this will sensitize you to how many there may yet be and prevent you from focusing in on the first thing that "sounds right" as The Truth. Disciplining yourself to think in this way—maybe *this* is happening, but on the other hand, maybe *that* is happening—keeps you from being rigid in your thinking, which in my tradition is considered to be extraordinarily counter productive.

Now you assign a personal probability factor to each explanation. This probability factor will be based on your personal experience. This is all you have to go on. Someone else's probability factor will be different because their experience is different. You will understand this. This is OK. It is inevitable.

Each of us has different experience and, therefore, different estimates of probability. This personal probability factor can never be 100%--and never, never 0%.

You see how it is? How all conclusions are wisely tentative, as new information may come in at any moment. Yet, whenever a decision is necessary, you can *instantly* and *clearly* select between your top three probabilities. All, we hope, above 95%! Decisions are, thus, enhanced and expedited, while the mind is kept alert to new possibilities.

∞

The Rule of Six: For the Right Side of the Brain (Written by Paula Underwood)

When I was even younger than I am now and brought my thoughts to my father, he would often say, "Remember the Rule of Six." Yes. The Rule of Six. So inculcated in my nature by now that I have great difficulty in naming only one thing as the root cause of anything else.

For life is like this: So many individuations acting and interacting at every identifiable moment, that nothing at all, no one thing, can cause anything else.

The Rule of Six says, "For every perceivable phenomena devise at least six explanations that indeed explain the phenomena. There are probably sixty, but if you devise six, this will sensitize you to the complexity of Universe, the variability of perception. It will prevent you from fixing on the first plausible explanation as The Truth.

And so it is, in a complex and changing world in which the past affects the future, but the future also affects the past, at least in that our understanding of the probable determines many of our decisions, provides signposts along many diverging, converging paths.

What we see when we open our eyes . . . depends on where we are standing at the time. Only move a little, to left, to right . . . gain the view from there. Tell me now, my Brothers, my Sisters, what does your New Vision show you? Move around the Circle of the Earth once more . . . and look again! A quarter turn to the left. A quarter turn to the right. Sit in the East and study life. Sit in the South and wonder. How is it to view the world from Moscow? Leningrad? Vladivostok? How from Durban? Cairo? New Guinea?

∞

We are all Earth's Children, and each view has value.

Now turn the Wheel on its edge, my Brothers, my Sisters. How is it now to view Life . . . as Wolf? As Eagle? As those with a Hundred Legs? Crawling, walking, swimming through Life . . . How is it now?

Complete the Circle in three dimensions . . . and then we will talk. - Kind Thoughts Come.

The Rule of Six and the Imagination (written by Judy Brown)

December 19, 2000

Today, Michael Jones, writer, pianist and composer and I were talking with appreciation and sadness of Paula's passing on December 2 of this year. And of her gifts and wisdom. I asked if he knew of the Rule of Six, and when he said "no," I sketched the idea, briefly. I said that usually, when we Westerners and non-Indigenous people come up with alternative explanations, it's in order to kill off all alternatives except the one "winning" alternative. Michael laughed and said that when the imagination senses that's the game, the imagination says "No way. I'm headed for the country for the day. Let me know when you're finished behaving like this." And so our alternative thinking lacks imagination. Paula's Rule of Six invites the imagination back into the game, into the creation of alternative perspectives and possibilities.

∞

Each day dawns

Each day dawns
With its own
Discoveries and surprises,
With its gifts.
If we are home
To all of that
We can't be lost.

∞

Ethics is Wrestling

Ethics
Is wrestling
With life–
The twists,
The sweat,
The strain–
It's not
The high jump
After all,
The race
Well run–
It is the mat
Upon the ground,
And shoulders,
And the
Struggle
To stay free.

∞

Some Questions for Ethical Dilemmas

Here are a series of simple questions I try to keep in mind to ask
when I am wrestling with an ethical dilemma:

> **Five questions (and their source) I try to
> remember to ask when I am wrestling with an
> ethical dilemma:**
>
> 1) Am I caring for the development of "the
> other," of that person or institution or cause for
> which I am the steward? Is my attention on the
> development of the "other" rather than on my
> own needs? (Read *On Caring* by Milton Meyeroff)
>
> 2) Am I telling the truth? Would I want to read
> about what I am doing on the front page of The
> New York Times, or in the headlines of my
> hometown newspaper? (Read *Lying* by Sissela
> Bok)
>
> 3) Am I listening for all voices, seeking all
> perspectives? Is the conversation broad
> enough to get at all dimensions of this
> dilemma? (Read *Who Speaks for Wolf* by
> Paula Underwood Spencer)
>
> 4) Am I selecting appropriate analogies and
> images for this dilemma? Particularly, as I think
> about historical analogies, am I being careful
> and thoughtful about my choices? (Read
> *Thinking in Time* by Richard
> Neustadt and Ernest May)
>
> 5) Am I trying to understand all the dimensions
> of the dilemma? Can I face the real complexity
> and sit with the challenge, or do I want to

∞

escape the complexity by doing a "slam dunk decision" and "winning"? (Think about Cone in the Box.)

Occupation

"Occupation?"
Says the woman,
Laughing,
At the window seat,
As the big jet
Prepares to land
In paradise.
She's helping her
Companion fill out
Immigration forms.
"Occupation?"
"Put 'Lover,' " she says
Laughing once again,
"Put 'International Lover.' "
He laughs, and with an
Accent, rich, adds,
"French Lover."
Laughing,
He fills in
The blank on the form:
"Hairdresser."

∞

Leading with Story

Recently I was asked to address a national group of state community mental health researchers about "Why research doesn't change the practice of the mental health profession," or as one of their leaders put it, "How come we keep having the same conversation and nothing changes?" "Why doesn't research change policy and thus change practice?"

My initial unspoken response to the question was, "We give folks the data, but we don't help them change their story." They have this startling or troubling data, on one hand, but the story they tell about how the world works, and how they work effectively within that world, and where they even fit into that world, is disconnected from the new data. There is a huge gulf between the data and their life, their values, their lived experience, and how they do things. No bridge is offered. Just the data and the research. The research and the data don't provide a new story, with room in it for them, so they stick with their old story, in the face of the data.

In talking with the researchers, I realized that the question they had posed was part of a much larger question, a fundamental leadership question: What makes it possible for individuals and organizations and institutions and movements—even entire societies–to be hungry for, and nourished by, data that shed light on the evolution and change that lies before, and around them, which is the very context for their lives and their work? Or put more simply: What makes change appealing, interesting, natural? How can the generation of new knowledge, of various kinds, contribute to that "natural" change while helping us to hold onto that which is appropriately stable and enduring?

As an educator interested in leadership dialogue and change, my life and my work with leaders across all sectors seems to be

∞

teaching me that transformational truth is more profound and multi-faceted than data alone, or even than the knowledge created from that data, can suggest.

Daily, we struggle with situations in which knowledge alone, and the mounds of attendant data, do not move people. Some wisdom traditions teach us that, "The truth will set you free." Still we have more and more data, and we seem to feel more and more stuck. Certainly not free. So where are we to find the truth that will move us–truth about our work and our lives–and how are we to speak of it to each other? How do leaders tap that truth and work with it?

I am learning that the kind of truth that sets us free isn't data alone. It seems to include the deeper principles of how things operate, the deeper principles imbedded within dynamic complexity and natural change. Truths of that nature, because they are both so rich and so simple, are often only communicable as story.

The story may be one person's experience (at least to begin with). Thus we see the use of circle processes of story-telling woven into conflict resolution processes. Or the story may be one that is archetypal–what Parker Palmer calls Big Story or what Carol Pearson's archetypes of fundamental human stories represent, or what creation stories in various wisdom traditions convey.

There seems to be something in a good story that can hold truth with simplicity, complexity and profundity at once. A good story has a kind of electricity to it, an energy that sweeps us along with it. And we end up in a different place within ourselves listening to that kind of story. As I have worked with organizations of all kinds over the decades, I have noticed that it seems mostly in telling stories that we have something that can be offered to others in a form that they can welcome, take in, digest, and which nourishes them.

∞

Story is genuinely invitational, an offering which the hearer can consider, but which is not forced upon them. It is the antithesis of the "sell," with its marketing energy seeking to influence and convince. Story simply offers. It is, as Herman Daly calls it, "unarmed truth." Or as I sometimes say to gifted engineers, it is the "stealth technology of communication." Story comes in under our naturally defensive radar, under the radar that says, "Don't you go trying to change my mind. I like my thinking the way it is."

So if this is true, then scientists who work to create knowledge out of data, and who frame the questions that we explore, must find partners among the story-tellers of our time. Only in a partnership between science and story-telling, among us and within us, can we begin to learn what we need to learn. Our scientists and policy-makers must tap the story-telling capacity within themselves, and around them, in order to tell the story that will guide us all in healthier, more life-affirming directions. Thus, I am advocating that each of us reaffirm the partnership around us and within us of the scientist and the story-teller.

There is a long tradition of concern that the community of science and the community of the humanities have not created strong enough bridges to link their ways of knowing. CP Snow and others have spoken eloquently of the need for that bridge. Others, like the paleontologist poet Loren Eisley, the medical essayist Lewis Thomas, Quaker economist and poet Kenneth Boulding, have embodied that bridge, providing us with rich advances in science and story at once.

So back with the mental health researchers, frustrated at the "stuckness" of doing more and more research, and finding that it changes little in the field of practice: Why is that so? And why is it so in so many places? Why do the manufacturing plants in which I have worked for years, tell each other what is needed to improve, and yet stay in the old patterns? Why do the headlines

∞

of our papers shout out our dissatisfaction with urban sprawl, yet we persist in codes and zoning and laws that spread it further, as if we cannot help ourselves despite what we think we know? Why do the symphonies with which I work, perform remarkable music in which they listen intently to each other on the stages of great concert halls, yet off-stage find it impossible to listen their way into a different set of relations between management and labor? I think the answer lies, somehow, in the bridging power of story. And in the absence of that bridge, data is without impact.

Standing before this sea of faces of mental health researchers, I realized that I live on that bridge. My friends at the Academy of Leadership call it the bridge of theory to practice, and the bridge back from practice to theory. My colleagues at the School of Public Policy where I teach leadership, call it professional education. The cooperative extension service which is the tradition in which I grew up, calls it extension education. Sometimes in my own life, it has been a solid bridge, sometimes only a rope bridge swaying in winds, a bridge nonetheless. It is perhaps in my DNA, as well as in the life I have chosen for myself, to serve the world from the bridge between science and story. And it is from that place that I began to explore with the researchers, the role of story in change.

Holding science and story, together; I grew up in a cooperative extension family, my father a soil scientist who headed cooperative extension for a rural northwestern Michigan county. My garden (I ran a road-side stand to earn college money) served as the university's experiment plot for testing new crops and new agricultural processes. The university's research faculty ("specialists," we called them) stayed at our house when they were visiting the county to meet with Dad and farmers. We lived 200 miles from the University of which my father was a part, and half a country from the United States Department of Agriculture which partnered with that University in cooperative extension and paid half of his salary. I grew up obliquely aware (as most

∞

children are obliquely aware of their parents) of the role my father played in translating and making accessible to farmers the scientific research that came out of the world of the University. And only recently have I come to understand how that translation had as much to do with story as with science. Much of that understanding came from a conversation with an old friend with whom I attended school from the time we were both five until we graduated high school. And from a photo that he showed me.

Marlo had stopped by to have a cup of coffee on my front porch, and to talk about his mother, the last of our four parents to die—to reflect with me about the end of her life and her passing. He had brought with him a picture taken by my father of his mother and father when they were farming the "home place," a potato farm on the south end of the county.

It was a classic black and white photo of two farmers, a man and a woman, in the early 1950's, standing at the edge of the field with the rows of potato plants stretching behind them into the distance. Stark. Powerful. He had found it among his mother's things after she died. And he wanted me to see it.

"I don't know how your Dad captured this," Marlo said. "He must have stood on top of the car to get this particular angle. The photo was really important to us. It seemed to me it was the first time we realized the remarkable thing we had accomplished with the farm and with our lives."

The poet in me was taken by the power of the photo, but even more by the realization that it was my father's artistry as a photographer (the framing, the angle, the light, the detail) that had given Marlo's folks hope and a greater sense of accomplishment. All those years, I had thought it was the science that was the contribution. Now I could see it was the art, the story that he had captured in the photograph. In a moment, my understanding shifted kaleidoscope-like as I looked at that photo,

∞

substituting an understanding of my father as scientist, with an understanding of my father as artist. It was a satisfying shift, pleasing. Simple. And as a poet, an artist myself, I felt this great comfort, recognition, affirmation in that understanding. "See," I said to myself, "It's scientist 'zero,' artist 'one.' Art wins."

Then I turned the photo over, and written carefully on the back of the photo were the following notations: "1952, acreage…planting date…rainfall….weather conditions…seed potato variety… planting conditions…prior year yield…." All the detailed and precise notes of the scientist. The data that was interwoven with the story.

In that moment, I realized there was no way to separate the two sides of the story. If I held the photo, I had to hold the contributions of both the artist and the scientist; I had to acknowledge that it was the scientist and artist together creating a new picture of what had been accomplished, and what was possible, in the life of one family. I sat with that photo in my hand for a long time. I think of it often.

It seems to me that leadership work is about just that: being a precise, disciplined and curious scientist and an aware and gifted story-teller. And not setting down one for the other, for it takes both habits of mind and both disciplines of spirit to find our path forward as individuals, institutions and communities.

We are required to make sure that we are able to offer a true and honest story that captures the emotional and spiritual richness that the data alone can't capture. This is not about "spin" or "marketing" or getting others to "buy-in" to a vision or story; this is about the essential truth of a complex reality that we can come to hold in common because it emerges out of the very fiber of our lives and experiences. It is about a story that is real enough, enduring enough, strong enough and supple enough, to carry our weight as we move forward. It is that kind of bridge.

∞

Story A and Story B at war within us and around us; But if a story can carry us forward, story can also hold us back from what our own lives are telling us. A story may blind us to the truth, as well as free us.

Thomas Kuhn's work on the nature of shifts in scientific understanding, and on how world view shifts in the scientific community gives us a window into that phenomenon explaining how hard it is to see the new "card deck," even once we intellectually know the answer. It's because we know how a card deck operates, and at some level we know there isn't a new deck in play—so our eyes have trouble seeing what's there. It's beyond intellect. It's believing that the game has changed.

Kuhn's idea is that believing is seeing. If we believe, we will be able to see what we could not see before. Because a story incorporates a belief system, it allows us to see the data. Or see it in a different light. The idea of a paradigm from Kuhn's classic work on the structure of scientific revolutions, suggested that often there are competing theories of how things work. For the most part the old theories hold sway, but sometimes a new theory captures the eye of the scientific community and they come to believe it (he uses the example of Copernicus) and the scientific community suddenly shifts to the new paradigm. Once that shift has occurred, then people find a way to measure the truth of that paradigm. Thus Galileo devised the telescope but only after the theory of Copernicus made it necessary to have it to measure the new theory. It's important to note that from one perspective the old truth still holds: the sun seems to circle us and sailboats disappear from sight on the ocean. But we now hold in our minds a larger perspective that teaches us that the conditions under which these truths prevail, and their meaning, are larger than we thought.

∞

Often in my work with organizations, and with individuals who are struggling to shift dynamics in their lives, I find there is an old story that has great power, that stands in unconscious yet powerful opposition to an emerging new story. And the old story keeps us from seeing the data in a way that could free us, could get us unstuck. My favorite story about that: several years ago, I was working with the operating committee of an electronics plant in the northeast. They were struggling with problems of quality and scrap in their product, and we were sitting around a big table, the plant leadership, another consultant, and myself, trying to sort out the problem. Trying to get unstuck and find a way forward.

"What's the problem?" I asked. "It's that group of laggards we hired a few years back," said one of the guys. "They are the problem. We were short of people and we just hired a lot of guys off the street and they have always been the problem. And the night shift is the worst. And the union is part of the problem too."

"OK," I said. "Just out of curiosity. How many folks around this table were union members at one time?" Most of us raise our hands. Me included. I was a teamster once. So both of the consultants and most of the current management were union members once, and yet they believe the union is the problem.

"OK," I said. "Just out of curiosity. How many folks around this table served on the night shift in a manufacturing plant?" Better than half raise their hand. Half of the management was once on the night shift. "OK. For how long?" (I'm figuring two or three months, maybe.) The answers: Two years. Five years. Eight years.

Now I am thoroughly confused. Here we have a group of folks in management who have <u>been</u> the very folks who they say are the problem. Even though they know they are no different from those folks. Interesting.

∞

We take a break. One of the guys takes me aside. "Funniest thing happened last month," he said to me. "All my supervisors were sick with the flu, and we absolutely had to run parts anyway, so I said to the guys on the night shift, 'Look, I am counting on you. You know how to do this. Just do your best.' " "So what happened?" I ask. "Well the strangest thing happened," he said, "The output went up and it stayed up. For days. Until the supervisors came back from sick leave. Then it went down again."

"Hm," I said to him. "What do you conclude from that?" His answer: "Well, it's obvious they can't sustain that kind of quality and productivity."

When I tell this story to the mental health researchers, they burst into laughter. Yet where there is a parallel story from their own work, they would see nothing funny in it.

"So what is going on in this experience"? I ask myself. Something important and profound. There is a powerful old story: the workers, and the nightshift and the union are no good and are the reason we can't do a good job in the plant, and it is the job of management to get them in line and to provide discipline to the workforce. That old story has such power that even the managers who have been in positions, during a good portion of their work-life, similar to the workers they are complaining about, discount their own experience in the face of the power of the old story.

Yet there is an alternative story that they catch glimpses of: "The production went up and stayed up. You know how to do this. Do your best." And the conclusion they draw from the experience of the breakthrough with the workers "self-managing" for several days is that "It's not sustainable." That conclusion is immediate because it is so habitual, ingrained, familiar. It is the powerful software of the old story that snaps them back, and it arranges the

∞

data so that there's only one possible conclusion: the old story of bad workers being the problem.

I am stunned by this experience, and I begin to listen more carefully for the presence of Story A and Story B in organizations. Suddenly I see those two opposing stories everywhere. I must think about what to do with this reality, as I see how the grip of Story A keeps folks from living into the truth of Story B even as the data makes Story B obvious and even though they insist that the new story, Story B, is what they long for.

Therefore, when we are stuck, we need to look for the bear-trap power of an old story (often a beloved one—in which we are special, or heroic, or chosen by God) which may be holding us back from the new and healthier story, the truth of which is right before our eyes, but we cannot see because we are captive of the soft-ware of the old story.

How do you work with story, particularly as a leader? Here are some starting points:

Help people gain practice in thinking in terms of story. I often ask, "What do you notice?" "What story do you tell yourself about that?" Such shifting between noticing and story, helps people gain a fluidity with story, and a consciousness about moving from data to story. It helps them realize the way in which a variety of stories can be constructed from data. And I use the actual word, "story" a lot.

Ask people to talk about their experiences in terms of story. Asking people the story of what brought them to this point in their work-life, or asking them to tell the story of a time when they were at their very best in the organization—such practices, within staff meetings, as part of getting acquainted with people, create a culture that is rich with story. They create the "story habit."

∞

When only Story A seems to exist, help people discover Story B.
Ask people what the essential story seems to be of what's going
on here. What is the story they tell about their organization, of
their place in it? Is that a healthy, life-giving story for the
organization, for them? Does it give them room to grow, achieve,
contribute? Or is it debilitating? I often ask if the story creates
options for them. Does it give them "wiggle room"?

Once people are aware of the story they are currently living, it
becomes easier for them to think about what the authentic
alternative story might be—the new story that is trying to make
itself heard here, felt here, the alternative story that is trying to
emerge. I ask what they are seeing that suggests a new story, the
beginning of another way of seeing. Where is that present?

Hold story as inquiry: While it is tempting as the leader, to
believe that the "story" carries the whole message, and that it is
the answer, it may be more powerful as a question than an
answer. There are intriguing stories of successful leaders who
have used story as a question. One Norsk Hydro Aluminium
plant manager began to hold the vision of the production plant as
a garden. That became his story of what it could be and what was
possible. But rather than simply tell that story, he spent time in
informal conversation with his employees, in small groups, asking
them what it would mean for them, and their work, if that story
were really true of the plant.

Karl Heinrich Robert, a Swedish medical doctor created the vision
of the Natural Step—a set of principles the Swedish people could
live by which would allow them to leave the earth better than they
found it. Rather than sell this alternative story of how his country
could live, he simply asked people, "Do these principles ring true
for you?" "Have I got it right?" "What would you add?" In the
dialogue about that question, the story became a society-wide
story.

∞

John Woolman, the early Quaker opponent of slavery, for many years walked up and down the east coast of the US asking slave-owning Quakers questions about what they would tell their children about what it means to be a Quaker who owns other humans. Long before the change came to any other place in the US, Quakers voluntarily gave up their slaves, became advocates for freeing all slaves and eventually were leaders in the Underground Railroad.

Make sure that the story has room for everyone. Here Martin Luther King is our model. The inclusiveness of his story of a society without segregation left room for everyone. It was a story about how the degradation of segregation tarnished the oppressed and oppressor alike. He realized that always the story, if it is to work for people, has to have room in it for everyone. There has to be space in the story for them. They must see themselves in it.

Respect and honor the end of the old story: I remember the wisdom of an engineering leader who held a ceremonial funeral for the old business and its old story. He had closed down the old original business unit, now outmoded, and the workforce had all been deployed to new settings. Yet everyone seemed stuck. Stuck in memories. Stuck in the past. So he chose to honor the memories and the past by holding a beautiful funeral celebration in the lobby of corporate headquarters, with music, and flowers, and speeches, and a casket. After that, finally, people could let go of the old story and move to the new one.

Sometimes honoring the end of the old story means incorporating elements of the old story in the new story. While it is tempting to want to entirely replace the old with the new, often elements of the "old story" need to find their way into the new story. Some folks will say including a bit of the past will help people "buy into" the change. I doubt that's what's at work: rather people are wise enough to realize that the unfolding future indeed carries important threads of the past. Over-emphasis by

∞

the leader on a story line that is "new" can deny this important reality.

A story is powerful if it is repeated; yet to have vitality it must remain alive and fresh for the story-teller, as well as those hearing it. I've often marveled at my colleague Michael Jones' skill as a story teller, and many of his stories are famous. We hear them again and again. Why aren't we bored by the repetition? I think it is because Michael himself is still learning from the story; it is still alive and powerful in his own life. And so we continue to consider its power in ours. In your own story-telling as a leader, be sure that the story you tell is vibrant, authentic, and one that is still alive for you.

Avoid the tendency to swing between the bad old story and an idealized new story. Remember all stories have their upside and downside. From the story of the development of the US interstate highway system, called "Divided Highways," I think of the woman who refused to let "Uncle Sam take her property" and bit the engineer who was going to put the road through her house. "She didn't bite me that hard," said the engineer on reflection. "I guess I would be upset too," he said "if somebody said they were going to take my home to build a road." But a transportation engineer, having watched this wrenching portrayal of the negative consequences of roads, said, "Roads will be part of our future; they are not the evil. People who designed the interstate system thought they were doing a wonderful thing, a monument to national security, engineering prowess and our courage and reach as human beings. It's just that now, we need a new story, in which roads are part of a larger picture of how we get about." There were tears in her eyes as she spoke.

Expand the reach of the story: Watch for chances to move the story beyond its limited domain to the larger domains where it has even greater leverage, reach and power, where it is desperately needed. This gives the organization the chance to live

∞

the story more completely, more fully. I remember providing dialogue training for symphony musicians and symphony board members, many of whom came out of the legal profession. Ironically, in their expert role both musicians and lawyers are highly skilled at listening. And yet when they had to work together, and with each other, they tended to tune each other out. So the "story" of what it means to have a widely successful musical organization had to be "stretched" beyond the listening and "attuning" that one sees on the musical stage and in the courtroom, into the story of how careful listening is central to the way the entire organization worked.

A colleague who had worked with the Cirque du Soleil organization, read a poem I'd written about the organization's dazzling performances. She said that what was remarkable was that the poem not only captured their performance, but also the way they worked together off-stage. That was an example to me of where the reach of the story had been expanded to encompass the entire life of the organization.

Create structures in which the new story is visible, manifest, real, inescapable: Sometimes it is necessary to create new visible structures, both physical and organizational, to make the new story visible and evident. And to hold it in place. One can see the impact of the visible structure of such a new story in the first of The Three Tenors concerts. It is the structure of the trio itself, the three stars no longer singing solo, that even without saying a thing makes it clear that a new story is unfolding. Placed within that structure the three sing the last word of the last song together. That last word: "Vincera" "I will win." Sung together. That's the new story.

Use all the power you have to live the new story and say "no" to the old story: Maryland's Governor Paris Glendening, an early proponent of better land use decisions, blocked a plan that the University of Maryland had developed to build a new western

∞

Maryland campus out on open farmland. The University insisted that as a University it had autonomy and freedom to do as it wished, and that it would be far cheaper to build on the farmland. The Governor held tight to the notion that he would not release state dollars to be spent by a state agency on a building that so violated the "new story" of intelligent land use. By laying down the law that folks could do what they wanted but where he had the power to draw the line, he was doing so, he made it clear that the new story was a serious story.

Use structures and practices that expand our ability to see many possible stories so we are not captive of one: Individuals and organizations can practice the skills of scenario building. The Rule of Six, the Ladder of Inference and similar mind stretches that keep us from falling into habitual stories. In a sense, dialogue itself allows us to see the many stories at work without seizing on one as the single right answer.

Avoid the corrosive danger of a story built on hatred and fear; instead create and uncover stories of common ground and attention to what matters most to us all: I end on this note, thinking of the research on optimism and pessimism: pessimists are right, but optimists seem to be much more successful and lead more satisfying lives. Our choice of story is our choice of whether to be an optimist or pessimist, of whether to live a story of fear or one of possibility and appreciation. Martin Luther King's choice of non-violence is a life choice. And the choice of story we tell, and thus live into, is a similar central life choice. It is an ethic— among political leaders, all of us. To lead from love, to tell stories from a position of appreciation, is not to in anyway diminish the truth at their heart, nor the sharp demanding edge of that truth, but it is an orientation toward life rather than death.

∞

Cirque du Soleil

Judy Br o w n

When I grew up
The circus
Had the animals
In cages,
The elephants
In lines.

Then even as that scene
Began to trouble me,
Emerged within our lives
A circus of a different kind:
No animals at all,
But humans with trapezes,
Trampolines and bicycles.
Instead of ropes and whips,
There were long flowing sheets
Of ruby-colored silk
From which the
Acrobats could swing.

What saved the animals?

Was it our seeing
What we'd done to them
And feeling bad?

∞

Or was it
That the beauty
Of a way
Of doing "circus"
So entirely new,
Swept us away,
And saved us from ourselves,
And saved the elephants
And tigers too?

Judy Sorum Brown, September 26, 2000, Dearborn, Michigan.

With a note of appreciation to the Montreal-based Cirque du Soleil, green architect Bill McDonough, ecological economist Herman Daly, Karl-Henrik Robert of Sweden's Natural Step, Betsy Taylor of the Center for a New American Dream, and legions of leaders everywhere who are helping us leave behind destructive practices by helping us discover a way of life more satisfying and beautiful than the one to which we have stubbornly and fearfully clung.

As Displayed in The Shambhala Institute's <u>Field Notes</u>

∞

Leonardo

If I read
My poetry
Out loud,
In public
Am I then
A poet?
Not a farmer,
Not a teacher,
Not a focused
Manager or
Leader?

But a poet?

Maybe you are
Leonardo,
He said,
Quietly.

∞

Shifts in Thinking, Creativity, and Breakthroughs

A shift in our thinking is learning. It means that we now see something differently than we did before. We make different meaning of data or an experience than we did before. Other words for this experience of shifting our thinking include "ahas," insights, breakthroughs, creativity.

Because we are natural learners, many such shifts occur naturally, and without much note. Sometimes we're almost unaware of them, and only on reflection do we bring them to a conscious level. At other times we may feel stuck, and want to consciously change our perspective or our way of thinking about a situation. We want to "think outside of the box."

All of us get stuck in our thinking and need to "break out of the box" from time to time. You might ask yourself, "What are the conditions under which I find it hard to change my thinking?" "And what are the conditions that make it easy or natural to change my thinking, to consider other ways of thinking?" We are always in some "box" or another (otherwise known as a framework) of thinking. The "box" is what helps us organize our experience. Getting out of it requires that we connect with our own center or essence, and that we listen deeply to ourselves. And it usually requires that we have the help of others, who by offering their experiences and inquiring into ours, help us to get clearer about what we perceive, and thus help us reframe what we are perceiving and step out of the box of our usual thinking.

A shift in thinking is an inner, private process that affects what is natural and easy for us to do. It is like changing our software so that the data is naturally arrayed a different way.

∞

Shifts in thinking, including those which produce a "discordant" idea, are a resource to the organization, to the team, but can be a resource only when shared.

Sometimes a shift in thinking can be unnerving, a little unsettling, as if we have lost our bearings for a moment. Perhaps the unsettledness is natural like the moment in neutral as we are shifting the manual transmission in a car. We may feel startled.

Learning or shifts in thinking, even in the most challenging of circumstances, are more likely if we perceive trustable structure and authenticity of relationship. That's why many learning experiences are marked by a learning structure that is solid and clear, (and perhaps unusual or non-habitual), and by a guide, teacher or learning partner who is authentic and connects with us.

What can we do that helps another person think out of the box?

- Inquiring, asking questions that come from a place of genuine not knowing;
- Listening with fresh ears, for what the person is saying. Listening to what might be underneath the words;
- Reflecting on our own experience and inviting the reflections of the other;
- Noticing;
- Wondering;
- Disclosing, particularly those things with which we struggle, which are dilemmas for us.

What seems to stop people from shifting their thinking — that is what stops them from learning, being creative, experiencing breakthroughs in their thinking?

- Judging;

∞

- Analyzing;
- Psychoanalyzing;
- Blaming;
- Dismissing and discounting.

These reactions seem to stop learning when they are communicated to the other person; they can even slow down learning and creativity, when one holds them as inner stances, when one is dismissive and discounting even in silence. That is why it is important to notice within ourselves when our inner response is one of judging, analyzing, blaming, dismissing or discounting, and to practice setting aside that response and choosing one that is more receiving of the others point of view. This is hard to do sometimes.

What are examples of learning structures that encourage shifts in thinking?

- Tracing Steppingstones and using other exercises that help us put our own experience in perspective;
- Practicing structured reflective writing;
- Asking and responding to questions that come from a place of genuine not knowing;
- Taking walks and talks as a way to break free of stuck thinking;
- Drawing–for example Marvin Weisbord's exercise of sketching, "My work as I see it; my work as seen by others; our organization as it is seen; our organization as I wish it to be";
- Changing the physical arrangement, for instance moving from rows of chairs into circles; remember all good work begins with rearranging furniture;
- Participating in dialogue processes that promote honest engaged conversation;
- Varying our mode of reflection among talking, visuals and physical activities;

∞

- Switching from intent to noticing, from what I want to create to what is emerging; switching back and forth between those two modes;
- Noticing intensity of feeling and inquiring into what lies behind the intensity;
- Listening to and telling stories. The structure of story and its metaphors open up new possibilities in our minds. Poetry, too, holds the power of metaphor;
- Noticing what I see and the story I tell myself. Moving from experience and data to story and back again. Asking what the assumptions are in the story I tell myself about the data;
- Engaging in physical exercises that parallel the dynamics that we are struggling with; Outward Bound, Chevreul's Pendulum, Circle on the Ceiling;
- Experimenting with Metaphor–Magic Eye Cards, Cone in the Box, toys that function as metaphor;
- Listening as an act of witness, including structures of Check-in and Check-out;
- Moving between fact-facts and feeling-facts, between thinking-thinking and feeling-thinking. Holding what one executive called a "right-brain meeting" and in place of the usual request for data, numbers and analysis, ask for feeling, sensing, levels of energy;
- Reflecting on music, video clips, short readings, quotes.

∞

Seed

Vision is seed,
The thing real
In a form
We don't yet see.
Not that we couldn't
See it
If we were
A squirrel,
A worm,
Or God.
An acorn is
As real a thing
As is an oak full grown,
A seed precisely like a tree
But in a different
Shape and time.
In seeds
Lie possibilities
And certainties at once,
Genetic maps of trees,
Small promissory notes of
A magnificence
That's yet to come,

Their outward
Size and shape
Still bearing no resemblance
To the vast and branching tree
They later will become.
Our dreams
And visions too
Are absolutely real,
As real
As what we now call real,
But they are in a different form,
As seeds within our lives right now,
Alive in every breath we take,
Yet in a shape we don't perceive
Or on a scale
That we can't yet recognize,
Unless like squirrels
We dig below the ground
And find the seed of promise,
Held in silence
For the time to come.

∞

There are Countries

There are countries
In our minds,
Whose boundaries
Keep thoughts
From crossing over,
Wondering.
No passports
To be had,
No possibility
Of exploration.

∞

Thinking about Paradigms, Frameworks, Mental Models and Strange Decks of Cards

Each of us, whether scientist, manager, engineer, or poet, works within a framework that is part of our training and our professional development. The framework provides us with an organized way of understanding the world around us, and a way of thinking about our work within that world. That framework is a combination of our science, our training, and our beliefs about the nature of our work. It is also part of our view of how the larger world works. The poet calls it our worldview. The scientist calls it our paradigm.

We don't generally think much about our framework—either the framework of our work, or of our broader world. We don't really need to think about it much, on a daily basis. In fact, to do the practical work of our life, we aren't required to think about it at all. Its rules are so basic as to be almost invisible to us. The framework "goes without saying," as we would say. It is the only environment and context we know. So we think it is the only possible environment. Often unseen and out of awareness, it is the backdrop for all we do. It provides the rules for our world. And therefore whether we are conscious of it or not, it shapes most of what we do.

As we work to understand, shape and lead organizations it is important, and very practical, to spend time early in the process getting clear about the foundation, or framework, upon which we are building the edifice of our work. The design of any organization is of course, built knowingly or unknowingly, on some foundation. The question is only whether or not we are aware of that foundation, and whether or not it is the best possible foundation for the effort we are undertaking. We almost never, in

∞

our rush to get on with the action, believe we have time for this kind of exploration. Yet without understanding the framework or foundation, we begin framing our efforts without any sense of the constraints or opportunities that foundation provides.

Such foundations, while they are foundations of ideas, operate consciously or subconsciously in a variety of very practical ways to organize reality for us and to help us make sense of information. Without such a framework, the world would be unintelligible to us. We would be in a situation analogous to the person who had been blind from birth and whose sight is restored during his adult years. Having never had sight before, his first perception is simply of disorganized swirling specks, unintelligible and without meaning. He has no framework for understanding that certain patterns of specks are faces, others are walls or the golden retriever that he knows so well by touch and smell.

So our frameworks organize data. And they provide tools for working with that data. As if a framework were a bag full of our most prized tools, we bring the framework with us where ever we work. We bring it to deliberations, dialogue, discussion and decision-making. We bring it to problems for which it is eminently well suited. We bring it to problems for which it is less well-suited.

As thoughtful leaders, it is helpful to become aware of the frameworks through which we, and others, view the world. That awareness increases our ability to perceive and respect the frameworks of others. It helps us use our own models of the world in ways which are most productive and ethical, and on those problems for which they are best suited. And it may alert us more quickly to instances where our framework limits our work in unacceptable ways, even though no new framework is emerging. At the very least, such awareness helps us simply know that we carry these bags of tools, and that they are not the

∞

only possible bags of tools to carry. Hopefully, our increasing awareness of frameworks can help us see early on when the paradigm within which we are working is beginning to disintegrate and is being replaced by a new emergent framework.

Although we are talking here of frameworks in the broadest possible sense–that of the scientific worldview–it is important to note such paradigms come to us from a variety of sources beyond science alone. For instance our disciplines and professions provide us with paradigms: most educators operate in the framework of a classroom and teaching. Most lawyers operate within the framework of the adversarial legal system. Engineers operate in a framework of design and test. Scientists operate within the framework of the scientific method, which is as the sweep of human history goes, a relatively recent development.

The most fundamental and long-standing of our frameworks come to us from the world of myth. Myths are the stories spun by our tribal imaginations over the centuries that humankind has been on earth, and represent certain underlying understandings of our role on earth. Even if we are seemingly unaware of these myths, our cultures tend to carry their message. Thus the Biblical story is cast within the framework of humankind driven from the garden, the slaying of brother by brother, and a great flood which allowed for a new beginning. The Greek myth of Odysseus frames human experience as a journey of exploration and self-knowledge. The Greek myth of Prometheus shows humankind as a failed project, only barely redeemed with the technology of fire, but still teetering on the brink of destruction. The story of Faust provides a framework of humankind's scientific endeavors as a source of hope as well as a deal with the devil. These myths are woven into our sense of what it means to be human, our view of our place in the universe.

Language also provides a set of subtle underlying frameworks which bound our understanding. Differences in language reflect

∞

culturally different experiences. In the simple example of which most of us are aware, an Eskimo language has a wide range of words to describe the various kinds of snow conditions. Spanish does not. French has the pronoun "on" which combines the concepts of "he" and "she." American English does not. Such differences bound our capacity to express nuance, and many would say, they bound our capacity to even perceive nuance.

History too, provides its own set of frameworks. We make meaning of the present by selecting from our past those experiences which seem to us to parallel and shed light on our current experience. We do this individually but also collectively, most visibly in public policy decisions and the choices of our public leaders. Neustadt and May in their classic book *Thinking in Time*, counsel us to become aware of these historical frameworks, and ensure that the framework we choose from our past indeed fits the current situation. The dangers of not doing so, they argue, are apparent in many of the failures of our own country's foreign policy.

And finally, the stories we tell ourselves provide frameworks. Bruno Bettleheim in his book, *The Uses of Enchantment*, notes how children's stories provide a paradigm, a framework, for small children who are trying to make sense of the world. As adults our stories about success and failure may play a similar role.

Even when we are unaware of the myths, language, history, and stories which are bounding our reality, they still hold power over us. One relatively new paradigm that shapes our actions and thinking is economics, and it was John Maynard Keynes, himself, who said that we are often captive of outdated frameworks:

> ." . . the ideas of economists and political philosophers, both when they are right and when they are wrong are more powerful than is commonly understood. Indeed the world is ruled

∞

by little else. Practical men, who believe themselves to be exempt from any intellectual influences, are usually the slaves of some defunct economist. Madmen in authority, who hear voices in the air, are distilling their frenzy from some academic scribbler a few years back. . . . soon or late, it is ideas, not vested interests, which are dangerous, for good or evil."

Against a backdrop of the frameworks of culture, myth, language, economics and history, is placed the framework of the scientific thinking. It is this framework, which the philosopher of science, Thomas Kuhn, described in his 1962 book, *The Structure of Scientific Revolutions*, and which changed fundamentally the way we understand scientific work. What interested Kuhn was how scientists work within a paradigm and how they shift to a new paradigm. How do they come to know that something is true? How does the work of scientists uncover new truths, new understandings of how the world operates? Kuhn's exploration of changes in scientific paradigms suggests that it is in the nature of things that experts, leaders, those with deep experience, are both helped and hindered by their knowledge and expertise. Although he wrote of the "hard" sciences, his observations hold as well for the social sciences, which form the explicit bed-rock of much national policy work and of our understandings of how organizations function.

Kuhn noted that rather than pushing back the frontiers of knowledge in a reasoned, regular way, scientists generally work only in a limited arena, within a set of parameters and rules. Within that paradigm, scientists do the work of "normal science." The paradigm within which the scientists operate sets the boundaries of scientific work much like the impact of a spot-light, which sheds much light on only a certain area allows us to see a great deal within that area. But while the spot-light illuminates one area, it does not bring to our

∞

attention data outside its ring of light. After a good deal of work has been accomplished within the existing paradigm Kuhn noted, a new paradigm begins to emerge.

Kuhn described the process whereby a new paradigm takes shape, and the tremendous upheaval experienced within the scientific community, as those working on the normal science see their life's work being called into question by a new paradigm. That new paradigm represents a new belief-set about what constitutes the work of science. That change in paradigm occurs, Kuhn argued, in a kind of perceptual flip, in which the scientific community, often influenced by the work of a renegade or maverick, comes to see things in a radically new and different way.

That different way of seeing includes different beliefs about what constitutes appropriate areas of inquiry, what kind of evidence is admissible in that inquiry, and what instruments might produce that evidence. In a sense, the new paradigm means that the spotlight of science is shown on different territory, or perhaps on a much broader territory, in ways that make new data available to us. Of course the data are not really new; they were there all along. But the spot-light of the old paradigm didn't shine on them. Thus, for instance, Einstein's work opened up a universe of the very small and the very fast. That universe was, until Einstein's work illuminated it, a universe that was off our scope, and world of data on which we had not yet shown the light of science.

Many paradigm shifts, including the earlier shift to Copernicus's sun-centered theory of the universe, take root at first on a theoretical level, before the data can be assembled to support the theory. Only when Galileo's work with the new invention of the telescope provided the data, was the theory Copernicus had advanced effectively proved true. The belief, however, that the

∞

sun, not the earth was the center of our universe developed within the learned community of science before the instruments existed to prove that theory. (Ironically, as a species–particularly those of us of Western rather than Eastern heritage–we have still not seemed to adjust our thinking to acknowledge that we are not the center of the universe.) The new science of chaos represents such a similar change in paradigm and one which requires the speed and capacity of new generations of computers in order to make data which support the paradigm manifest.

Now, thanks to Kuhn and his popularizers, we are excruciatingly aware of paradigms. Every slight shift in perception gets termed a "paradigm shift" and we are exhorted to "shift our paradigms" on a regular basis as if our frameworks were some kind of fancy sports car. Such exhortations often fail to realize what Kuhn so clearly saw: our relationship to a paradigm is not wholly an act of our own will, or a matter of choice. Rather the perceptual shift involved in a paradigm shift may be almost wholly involuntary, like that which Kuhn describes in the classic card deck experiment.

In this experiment, cards from a card deck are flashed before the viewer, one at a time, at first very fast and then slower and slower still, and the viewer is asked to take notes on what the cards are. But these cards are not all the standard cards from a deck so familiar to us. Some, like a red spade, or black heart, are "abnormal, odd, weird."

When we show the cards to people, they usually get the right cards right. But they are confused, thrown off by the odd cards. "Something is wrong," they say. Or they simply read the "odd cards" as if they were the usual cards: Their mind turns a red spade into a heart. Their experience and expectations of a card deck limit their ability to see what is right in front of them. What happens when we make it easier to identify the cards? Do they appreciate having more time to look at each card? Do they note

∞

them correctly? No. Given more time, they become more
confused. Or they just get mad, becoming more and more put out
with the person running the experiment, and exposing them to the
cards. More upset.

Even when one knows the "trick" ones eyes still tend to see the
right cards fast and to have trouble perceiving the "wrong" cards.
What does all this suggest? It certainly suggests that intellectually
knowing about a new paradigm doesn't ensure that we can live
into it and see the data easily or correctly. And it reminds us that
much about our relationship with paradigms is beyond our
control. Often, as in the case of Einstein, the breakthrough
thinking comes from the fringe. Einstein was toiling away in the
Swiss patent office, not able to get an academic appointment when
he wrote the theory that would change our understanding of the
world. And it suggests that breakthrough insight operates almost
as a belief system shift, a kind of tipping point of thought that
allows the scientific community to finally follow the theory that,
in the case of both Einstein and Copernicus, was no more
provable on the basis of data than the dominant or alternative
views of the time.

There is a certain "swept away" quality to the process of a
paradigm shift that dismays the logical among us. Even the great
scientists whose work broke with an old paradigm (Copernicus,
Darwin, Einstein) and who realized that they had broken with the
scientific past in a fundamental way, found it hard to let go of the
moorings of that past. Einstein's insistence that, "God would not
play dice with the Universe," represents his discomfort at
exploring the full implications of the new paradigm that he has
unleashed. He had difficulty embracing a probabilistic god and
letting go of the familiar, historical, deterministic god, whose
existence has been shattered by his own theoretical breakthrough.
There is a period of transition between paradigms which leaves us
all feeling strangely adrift, as if a new pattern exists but eludes our
consciousness.

∞

We must acknowledge that when the new paradigm becomes apparent, it not only changes how we perceive the universe and our role in it, but it carries with it a new set of understandings about the basic nature of causality—of the links between and among phenomena in our world. That change of understanding of the nature of causality is central, then, to how we approach problem solving. For example, the scientific paradigm of the world of Newton's universe, suggested that if you push down on a lever in a certain way, you will get a reaction of a certain magnitude—every time, in the same way. His paradigm has an implicit model of causality, and by extension, an implicit model of how you stop something from happening. A paradigm different from Newton's, has a different causal model. The world of the science of chaos for instance, suggests that in a whole range of complex phenomena (such as weather, and river eddies, and perhaps human relationships), causality is not a straight-line matter but rather a result of complex and probabilistically defined feedback loops, in which a small initial action can produce vast impacts, or sometimes, no impact at all. One way to describe this world is in terms of the "Butterfly Effect"—the theoretical possibility that the action of a butterfly flying in a distant portion of the globe can put into motion a series of events resulting (in a certain understanding of the concept of "results") in a hurricane in North America.

Some of us can probably think of instances in which, as a leader, or a family member, or a manager, we have indeed behaved like the butterfly and produced a hurricane. Or on the other hand, we may have used what we thought was a lever on a system which we believed obeyed Newton's laws, only to realize there was no impact from our pushing the lever. Much of what we encounter as frustration as leaders, and particularly policy leaders, comes from mistakes in our understanding of the nature of world in which we are trying various levers. We use what is supposed to be a predictable lever which will produce predictable

∞

results. Sometimes it works. At other times, nothing happens at all. Still at other times, the results are massive, but unexpected.

What is causing all this? Perhaps " 'Tis our thinking makes it so"– our ways of processing what we see in the world, the soft-ware of our frameworks is making it hard for us to operate in wise ways in our world. It is at such times, when things that should work don't seem to work, that we may be caught in a change in paradigms. And at such times, we are more likely to be successful if we are aware of our own paradigm and of possible competing paradigm structures.

Since part of our paradigm is the result of the scientific thinking of times earlier than our own, an important step as a leader in any enterprise, is to develop some understanding of those scientific frameworks, and what they suggest about causality. As Fritof Capra would remind us, the scientific paradigm silts down. It seeps into the understandings of a wide range of human endeavor, in a slow, uneven process. This means that today's patterns of thinking reflect unevenly the scientific paradigms which were dominant in the world of basic science hundreds of years ago. We can see these uneven shifts in frameworks across the worlds of biology, music, and art. We can see a shift in poetry in the difference of form between the time of a Shakespearean sonnet and e.e. cummings' poems. We can see a shift in the world of music between the regularity of Bach and the innovation of Stravinsky. And this has ever been so, just as the science of hundreds of years before Shakespeare is reflected in the language of his poetry and plays:

> "The heavens themselves, the planets, and this center,
> Observe degree, priority, and place,
> Insisture, course, proportion, season, form,
> Office and custom, in all line of order."
>
> (*Troilus and Cressida*, I,iii,85)

∞

And if the poetry of Shakespeare reflects an earlier science, the science of Shakespeare's time probably is reflected in the Twenty First Century arrangements of the assembly line and the school year.

In a dismaying process, at least dismaying to the logical among us, it seems that the new instrumentation, measurement and proof follows rather than precedes, the shift in paradigm. And often long after the scientific community itself has shifted, other related disciplines are still following the old familiar thought pattern of a discredited way of thinking. This tendency of the rest of the world to be stuck in the older way of thinking, while science itself has moved on to a more powerful paradigm, is the message of the Liv Ulmann movie *Mindwalk*, in which a scientist, an ex-patriot American poet, and a failed candidate for the US presidency take a long walk around the French island of Mont St. Michel trying to make sense of their own struggles in the world.

And finally, we come to realize that even when human minds shift, it takes still longer for the institutions, the bricks and mortar formed around the old way of thinking, to make the shift. We are frustrated by the slowness of change in many of the fixed shapes of institutions (conceptually and physically). They remain captured by the old notions, unable to see and to accept what the scientific community may have grasped years, decades, even centuries earlier.

My favorite example of such frustrating lethargy: I remember my shock at reading the 1992 front page story in the New York Times announcing that the Vatican had, on the previous day, acknowledged that Galileo was right about the earth revolving around the sun: "Si muove." The earth moves. The public institutional recognition of that shift by the Catholic Church occurred over 300 years after the theory had been proven..

∞

While it is true that the perceptual flip which is part of a paradigm change is not voluntary, a paradigm shift does not leave us without choices in our actions. The paradigm may have a life and logic of its own. But we are faced with decision-points about the kind of world that we build within that paradigm. In fact, it is often the paradigm-breaking scientists who argue most heatedly for responsible choice on the part of humankind. That was certainly true of the scientists who ushered us into the atomic age. The new paradigm doesn't absolve us of responsibility, it only changes the nature of that responsibility.

Nor does the new paradigm sweep away all our basic values— values like truth, caring, responsibility, freedom, and equality. Those values remain. Rather the new paradigm calls upon us to think in fresh and deep ways about how such values are to be reflected in the work done within the new paradigm. The old operational definitions of those values generally don't fit the new paradigms. For instance, for Aristotle, and to a large extent Thomas Jefferson, the idea of liberty applied to all, except women and slaves. In our time, thankfully, the meaning of liberty has been vastly expanded.

Some take-aways from all this:

The more expert, and experienced, and schooled we are in a field, the less likely we are to see the aberrant data that suggest our theory or paradigm or worldview is limiting us. Being smart is no protection against this limitation. Being in charge is no protection against this limitation. Being experienced is no protection against this limitation. In fact all three may all be liabilities. This is a heads-up to smart, experienced, expert leaders.

When somebody patiently slows down the aberrant information so we can see it, we are likely to get mad at them. We do not see what does not fit the story we are telling ourselves about how things operate.

∞

In fact, we either get mad at the person who brings the information, or we distort it to fit our preferred story.

Often it is easier for those completely outside of a field to see the way our paradigm is limiting us. That's what causes them to say, "Why in the world do they do that...? Why that way...?"

Long after a model we love and use, has been discredited in its own arena, we are likely to hold onto it for its familiarity and use it as a model or a way of thinking in other areas. Thus, for instance, fascinated by the Newtonian mechanical clock-work model, we still think of organizations as machines rather than as ecological, dynamic, human systems.

How can we think outside of the box of limiting paradigms? I believe it takes three things to break out of the box:

- It takes awareness of the way the mental processes work and a wariness and suspicion of our own certainty.

- It takes personal and collective disciplines that stretch our thinking and our minds.

- And it takes exposure to many other points of view and ways of knowing, including those that our old logic tells us are non-scientific, irrelevant, without merit, and "beside the point." Those have the most chance of dislodging us from the certainty that limits our ability to be effective in the world.

And some final conclusions:
First, frameworks come to us from a variety of sources: professional training, myth, language, history, story, and science. Second, we tend to be unaware of our own frameworks and thus oblivious to the ways they shape our work. And if we are

∞

unaware of our own, we are even more oblivious to those of others. Third, scientific paradigms impact the thinking, in a trickledown fashion, of a wide range of human efforts, so all of us, scientist and non-scientist alike, are well served by some basic understanding of those frameworks. Fourth, debates in our institutions as well as in the broader society—about the nature of the problem and the most likely solution—as well as debates about whether and why solutions have failed in the past, have underlying them one or another framework of the kinds discussed above, on which the policy edifice and debate of the day are knowingly, or unknowingly being constructed. As thoughtful leaders, we have a responsibility to dig away at that hidden foundation so that we and others can be more aware of the shape and the constraints of the foundation on which we build our work.

The Bridge with a Sign

He had found
A bridge,
With a sign:
"Please use
this bridge
to cross."

He wondered aloud
How many times
In his life
He had wandered
On the bank
Of a river of change,
And not seen
Such an obvious sign,
Nor put his
Foot upon the bridge
Before him.

∞

Experiments in Mind Shift for Transformational Leaders

In the midst of the challenges of leadership and life, often we have to give up old mindsets and experiment with new ways of thinking. Here are a series of those shifts that can make a dramatic difference in the effectiveness and the satisfaction we find in our work.

1. Let go of the notion that you'd be a better leader if you had better people.

Grab hold of the notion that **the only thing you have to work with, that you <u>can</u> change, is yourself.** I suspect the continual judging of others as insufficient to the task, flawed, is something folks can sense, can almost smell. And they run from it, not toward it. The question is not, "Can they do it?" The more actionable question is, "How must I change the conditions I am creating as a leader in order to increase the likelihood of their being able to do what they are capable of doing?" "Under what conditions can they do it?" "How do I as a leader, create those conditions?"

2. Let go of the notion that the good leader must have a complete plan thought through, must be able to chart the entire course, to see the entire path opening ahead, must have a plan, finished, completed, that others will buy into. Knows how to achieve the goal. Give up the idea of first planning and then doing.

Grab hold of the notion that the leader creates conditions where it is possible for folks to go, together with the leader, to places nobody has gone before. Set aside the old mindset: "As a leader I think and plan, and then I talk, and then they do, and then I judge." Experiment, with a mindset of, "I engage them in

∞

thinking and planning a forward step, and together we work on that step. Then we assess our progress and we see what we've learned, and we chart another forward step." **This is a thinking-talking-doing-learning all together at the same time form of leadership.** It is not the leader as field marshal, or supreme commander. It is the leader as lead scientist with a team of action researchers. It is the leader with a group of explorers. It is expeditionary learning. It is leading a fishing trip where you have to catch fish in order to eat.

3. Let go of the belief that if you are confused, you need to analyze things until they are clear.

Experiment with the notion that **good leaders respond to confusion with questions**, inquiry, drawing others into a conversation. It is inquiry and conversation that remove confusion, not solitary brilliance.

4. Let go of the belief that the leader is fearless.

Consider that **the effective leader is aware of her fears**, open about them and moves forward nonetheless. She is someone folks are more likely to trust, to travel with.

5. Let go of the belief that the wise leader only seeks information from certain trusted sources, and looks for answers in only certain relevant disciplines and fields.

Experiment with the notion that **the effective leader tries to learn from everywhere and everyone**. This leader is marked by insatiable curiosity, and the ability to ask questions that draw people's thinking out. Ask yourself: "From whom do I think I cannot learn?" If you find that you cannot learn from certain individuals or from certain types of people, then ask yourself this question: "What treasured view of myself requires that I cannot learn from this person?"

∞

6. Let go of the belief that when there is a crisis, or that when things are particularly serious, it is best to draw the wagons close. Let go of the notion that crisis is not a time to get outside perspectives, nor to experiment.

Experiment with opening out and increasing participation and perspectives in the midst of crisis. I learned the value of this shift in mindset by working with a colleague who led 52 successive and successful efforts of SWAT teams to free hostages without a shot being fired. Later he headed the Maryland State Police. Together he and I taught executives the importance of working against the habit of becoming closed and secretive in crisis. (I also learned something about fun being part of serious business when he told me that at the suggestion of one of his troopers, he experimented with putting fake cardboard police cars on the median of Interstate 95 to slow down drivers. It worked. Cheap and effective.)

7. Let go of the notion that when things are going well, we have learned what we need to learn.

Consider instead that when things are going well, we may not know why, and when they go awry we may then be too upset to learn. **Instill a discipline of regular learning from success and set-backs,** from breakthroughs and dead-ends. Since people tend to grand-stand about wins and deny losses, learning from either doesn't occur naturally, so leaders must build in processes of mindset and structure that ensure learning from experience.

8. Let go of the notion that the good leader is a visionary who can get others to buy into his vision.

∞

Instead, grab hold of the notion that **the effective leader engages**, and taps the courage and confidence of those around him, by helping them articulate and hold in common a vision of the possible which has real meaning to everyone, including the leader.

9. Let go of the notion that the leader must be either visionary or realistic.

Instead adopt the mindset that the power of vision comes not from vision alone, but from the ability of the leader to engage folks in honest conversation about why the vision matters as well as what they see as practical current reality, and what they are going to do about it. When a leader can talk candidly about vision and current reality, folks see in the leader, and strengthen in themselves, the ability to have high aspirations and to take in reality too. And to talk honestly about both. **The powerful leader is one who can take in reality** and shift thinking, without shifting persona, values, and vision. Folks will walk a long tough road in such good company.

10. Let go of the notion that the leader whether controlling (that is, micromanaging), or empowering (that is, hands-off), exacts promises or a commitment, and waits to judge whether or not folks produce. That's digitized leadership: right/wrong, good/bad, did it/didn't do it, winner/loser, etc.

Instead grab hold of the notion that **the leader engages colleagues in a conversation** and travels with them where that conversation leads, continually, repeatedly (boringly) asking key questions that move them forward in the work. My key questions are:

What are we trying to do here?
What's the plan for moving us forward (getting us unstuck, or making a breakthrough)?

∞

What are you seeing as we move forward?
What sense do you make of what you are seeing?

These four questions, cycled through again and again, help folks move forward.

11. Let go of the notion that the leader is in the position because she has superior knowledge or skill, is in a class by herself, and will finally help us do what we need to do.

Experiment with the notion that **the leader is now the person in a stewardship position** in this organization, gifted and limited by his own experience and knowledge, and dependent on the talents of those around him to see the whole picture. This mindset gets folks out of idealizing or demonizing leaders, (or first idealizing them, and then when they turn out to be human, demonizing them). It's hard to listen to your own wisdom with someone you idealize and its hard to learn from someone you demonize. Neither one is a good option if you want to learn fast. Best to stay on the human-being to human-being level.

12. Let go of the notion that being seen as a leader who is professional, competent and accomplished, means being dispassionate, unemotional and objective.

Experiment with the notion that **the powerful leader is real, present, honest about learning** from set back and breakthrough, vulnerable, has a life, and is honest, open, and genuinely, naturally emotional about what matters most.

13. Let go of the notion that strong feelings, conflict, intensity and setback are a block to the work, and must be either worked around, or vented, in order to get folks to a place where they can do the work that needs doing.

∞

Instead, experiment with the notion that learning through strong feelings, conflict, intensity and setback are the work calling to you as a leader. They are guidance about where to go with your energy and attention, not to clear the emotions or conflict up or fix them or eliminate them, but to inquire into them, and to help folks focus that emotional energy laser-like on the purposes of the organization. This mindset allows you to **see emotion as energy** waiting to be focused on meaningful work, and as evidence of what matters most. And as evidence that folks are alive. The gifted leader goes to the place of that intensity to learn what is to be learned and to tap and focus the power of that intensity.

14. Let go of the notion that the personal and the professional have no place together.

Consider that **the personal can give us glimpses into the professional capacities, can help us see the gifts of the other,** and perhaps may help us reflect those gifts back to that person in ways they themselves had not seen. Consider that the best results can often come from modeling and encouraging a sense of wholeness, of life divided no more. This allows folks to be honest about who they are and what's going on in their lives. It allows them to bring the wisdom of outside interests into the work place, to have integrity at work, and full identity. That's the reason a plant manager would begin the work at an off-site by asking everyone to check in with the answer to this question: "What's the most significant thing that happened to you last year, and what impact has it had on you?" Honest responses about great difficulties, set-backs, and challenges provide folks with a greater understanding of each other's strengths and experiences and build new respect and compassion. It leaves people with greater faith in each others' courage and capacity.

When a leader tells me of the value in his life of a certain place he can sit and think, in nature, I know I am working with someone

∞

who **knows how to keep himself balanced**, who knows what
matters most, who has perspective. And I know he will probably
not get wildly off balance. So I am able to follow his leadership
with confidence. What matters most to each of us, even in our
personal lives, says a lot about our capacities, and that says a lot
about what we can do in business.

15. Let go of the notion that leadership work is telling folks what
they need to do for you, and how you want them to do it.

Experiment with the notion that **leadership is asking folks what
they need from you.** To do superlative work for the customer,
And then doing what they ask to the best of your ability. This is
what this looks like in action: One production team explained
how they were able to hit impossible production numbers—real
breakthrough. "It was simple. We had an electrician we could
trust and he fixed things. And we had a boss, who whenever we
ran into a roadblock *we* couldn't remove asked us what help we
needed and took care of the problem. We did the rest. It was
simple."

16. Let go of the notion that an empowered workforce requires a
boss who doesn't intrude with her point of view, or expertise—a
hands-off leader.

Experiment with the notion that **folks are hungry for your
perspective**, your expertise, your knowledge, your leadership.
And make sure you offer it generously but with clarity and
honesty about its sources and its limits. A leader operating in this
way says, "The perspective I bring to this problem comes from
my experience in . . . or my training in . . . or my faith in the
engineering wisdom of . . . ." Such framing makes clear that your
perspective is not meant to trump other wisdom, but to stand
beside it. And it also helps folks understand where you gained
that perspective, which experience provided you that
perspective. They need to know your thinking, not just the

∞

judgment that is a result of your thinking. This kind of leadership also reflects an understanding that if we want an engaged workforce, we must shift to being engaged leaders. Engaged with the workforce and with the work.

17. Let go of the mindset that once a solution is engineered it is set, no matter what.

Consider an experimental mindset. **We are learning our way forward**, conducting intelligent and careful experiments, paying close attention to the results.

18. Let go of the idea that the hard truths are too hard for folks to hear, and must be mixed with a little "sugar and spice."

Consider the possibility that **folks need and welcome candor**. But realize that a call for candor is not a request for harsh treatment. Candor and honesty about tough realities can be delivered with compassion and empathy. If folks are to seek and welcome candor, **it must be offered as a gift** which presumes good will on everyone's part, not as a shot at them. And they will also appreciate the leader's honesty about his own struggles with those tough realities. This is not time for a "I know this is hard on you...." speech, but rather words like these: "Here are some tough realities I am discovering. Here's how I am struggling with them. I expect they are going to be a real challenge to us all. Let's talk about that." Experiment with a more open sharing of what you are seeing. At the same time be clear about the many meanings that could be made of what you are seeing, and that your interpretation is one of many possible.

19. Let go of the notion that a real leader stays above the fray of the day to day work, doing only thinking, planning, leading and strategizing.

∞

Consider instead that **the most gifted leaders lean into the work,** going to its heart, hands on and all of self in the work, to encourage, learn, understand, teach and do. I see this mindset in the plant managers I know who are out on the floor regularly, even on the night shift, talking with folks about the future of the plant. I see it in inner city principals who walks the hallways encouraging students and colleagues, following up on earlier conversations.

20. Let go of the notion that de-motivation, inaction, and stuckness must be overcome by leadership energy—as if low performance is a form of resistance to be overcome by the force of the leader's superior energy.

Consider, instead, that **the work of leadership is to sense the energy flows in the system,** and inquire into blockages, acknowledging the realities, asking where folks are feeling stuck, and immediately going to work removing those blockages so that the natural flows of energy and productivity in the organization are reopened.

21. Let go of the notion that folks need direct negative feedback in order to grow, change and improve.

Consider the notion, that like teaching a child to ride a bicycle, it's more a matter of **noticing what they are doing right,** by saying "Yes, that's it. You're doing a great job of peddling steadily. Good balance. Keep moving like that." Give up saying "Don't fall over. Last time you had a hard time. Don't do that."

22. Let go of the notion that if it's a good idea, it's good for everybody, everywhere, all the time. That's the notion of the roll-out, the blanket approach.

∞

Try out the "uniqueness" approach. What might be uniquely powerful here? Are there other places it might also work? Where? What about it is applicable elsewhere?

23. Let go of the idea of fixed priorities, objectives.

Try out the idea of **leverage as a beginning point** for having the most impact. "What do we know now that would suggest the most powerful and useful place to begin?" In dynamic systems, however, leverage can move. So keep learning about the impacts of what you're doing. What would make the biggest difference right now? In the long-run? What action carries the biggest wedge of payoffs across the system?

24. Let go of your sense that action is a matter of doing.

Consider that **action is often a matter of reaching out**, asking, wondering with someone. Action is often a matter of speaking truth to power. Action is often a matter of walking across boundaries and making common cause. Action is often a matter of being curious about the roots of conflict.

25. Let go of the sense that ultimately it is all up to you.

Consider the possibility that when you feel uniquely responsible, you might ask "**Who else do I engage in this challenge?**"

26. Let go of the mindset of seeking the single root cause.

Try to look for interconnected tentacles of casualty. The leaders and researchers of yesteryear focused on discrete isolatable cause and effect including a focus on how her leadership by itself makes a difference, is different from all others, is different from the person before. In that mindset a good leader left an indelible mark. Today's leader needs to look for interconnected tentacles of

∞

casualty, the way issues link together in patterns across many levels : energy, thinking, money, physical set-up, business plan.

27. Let go of the belief that you know how to think about this situation that is such a challenge, and consider that perhaps the way you are thinking about it is the problem.

Practice a conscious search for alternative mindsets. Some leaders do that by bringing in outsiders with all different backgrounds. Others do it by drawing out folks' experiences that lie outside of the day-to-day work. Either way it is a search for new mindsets that might work better in the current situation.

28. Let go of the notion that everything depends on your performance on this job, at this plant, with this boss, in the face of this challenge.

Try a mindset instead that **as a leader you have a life-work**, a purpose, a mission, and that today you are doing that life-work in this setting, with as much passion, and skill and grace as you can muster. This is how you are living your purpose now.

29. Let go of the search for opinions and judgment and assessment of the "problem."

By naming something the "problem" we change our relationship to the situation. **Try seeking perspectives** on the situation, on the development, on the dynamic.

30. Let go of the belief that folks must see you as strong, certain.

Consider that we may learn the most from each other's human vulnerabilities. And **it may be our vulnerabilities as much as our strengths that allow others to follow us with confidence.**

∞

31. Let go of the notion that the leader works with just three thing: physicals, financials and head-counts.

Consider that the raw material of leadership includes human heart and spirit, language and meaning, and the power of the connections among the physical, financial, strategic, emotional and spiritual (energy, creativity, joy, fun). If you can pull those together into a single coherent story, then you will have given folks a field on which to do great work.

32. Let go of the notion that the business leadership and the business smarts, are at the top of the organization.

Grab hold of the notion that **there aren't very many folks in your organization who couldn't run a small business** (in most places some do so and on company time) or at least a household (most all are doing so). If that's true, why in the world wouldn't you get all these business minds working on information about the business and how its doing?

33. Let go of the notion that the leader must exert control over the organization's actions.

Instead **lead so you increase the creative capacity of the organization**, its ability to create value, whether it's in the control plans or not. This work is all about getting great results rather than staying in bounds. The only bounds of the organization that are sacrosanct are its core values.

34. Let go of the notion that all change produces resistance. It is true that change the way we usually do it produces resistance, but that is more a statement about how we think things have to be done, than about the inherent nature of change and the inherent nature of the human species.

∞

Ask yourself what change in your life has been natural and welcome. Ask others that question. Listen to the answers. Shift your mindset from change as a disruptive, unwelcome, necessarily forced, to change as insight, invention, breakthrough, freedom, getting unstuck, learning. **All learning is just a change of mindset. Ask how change could develop in those more natural learning ways.**

35. Let go of the notion that the leader is always a good soldier who expects good soldiers beneath him. Or alternatively that the leader is always a renegade, standing in opposition to the forces above him.

Instead consider this mindset: **The leader shows courage and persistence** in balancing local and system needs, in balancing advocacy and inquiry, in balancing short-term and long-term needs, in balancing the needs of the existing base of the operations with the needs of the emergent business. The leader always moves in relationship to leaders above, beside, below. The leader listens to all voices, inside and outside the organization, for what they offer as wisdom in moving the organization forward. The gifted leader is one who sets her own balance among these inevitable tensions. Leadership is neither about blind obedience, nor open disregard, but rather about balanced integration of a set of claims upon the organization.

36. Let go of the mindset that the purpose of the numbers is to judge.

Shift to thinking of numbers as a source of constant learning, most useful to those closest to the work. **Lead by the numbers and put emphasis on getting good numbers to those who can move those numbers.** Engage folks in the process of deciding what numbers they need in order to produce better results. Focus on data for learning at the local level rather than data for bosses to judge workers. Ask: "What data do you need to do

∞

your job in the best possible way?" Get it for them, no matter what.

37. Let go of the idea of settling for the numbers that you've always used or that are easy to get.

Try a **focus on getting folks data on what really matters to them** and to their effectiveness including simple indicators of a wide variety of dimensions: data on feelings, perspectives, financials, physicals.

38. Let go of the idea that somebody else is making the rules about numbers.

Make your own rules about the numbers. Choose those that have the leverage you need. In doing so, be explicit and honest about the ways that data for judging (judging people's performance or group performance, or organizational performance) prepared for those in power (the bosses) shuts off the data for learning, or data that might be self-motivating (like stretch goals). When the bosses want to know how things are going in order to judge things, everybody stops learning and starts preparing presentations that are for the most part political and remarkably silent about the lessons from setbacks. Might as well admit this is true, and manage the reality. Where necessary keep the two kinds of data separate.

39. Let go of the mindset that only the leader can determine which numbers have leverage on folks' behavior and productivity. And that leaders make these determinations and then manipulate people's behavior with them.

Consider instead that if you **ask folks which numbers will help them manage**, which numbers motivate them, they will have some good ideas. Ask folks how <u>they</u> can keep the simple data that they need to do a better job. Let them do it. Let them

∞

experiment with how to keep simple track of solid numbers that help them make a difference in performance.

40. Let go of the mindset that the more data the better, and that when you have numbers, you have truth.

Instead **focus on the essentials** and consider that data is not knowledge much less wisdom. Knowledge is what comes out of thoughtful conversation about the data. Wisdom is what surfaces when many folks can bring their whole experience to that conversation. Up to the point of a collective conversation, all you have is data. If the collective conversation is just an analysis of the data to reach a judgment, without running it through the wisdom of folks' hard won experience, it is just knowledge—but un-integrated. Go for the wisdom. For the learning. Ask "What is the data we see? What sense do we make of it? What story do we tell? What are alternative stories? What does our own experience bring to bear on this?"

41. Let go of the idea that what matters is resolving a crisis, fixing things, being quickly responsive, dropping everything for the customer (or the boss).

Consider that what matters most is establishing and maintaining **a web of relationships** in good repair and a train of thought on a track that is going somewhere.

42. Let go of the idea that some folks "get" this new kind of leadership. Others just don't "get it."

Consider that **we all get it to some extent, and lose it under certain conditions.** One executive said just that: "It's not that some folks get it and others don't. It's that I get it, I get it, I get it, and the third day I lose it. Then I remember it. Then I lose it again, and you remind me. It's more like that." One leader may lose it every third week, and end up screaming at his folks on

∞

the floor. "I just blow my fuse," he says to me. Yet he never loses the dimension of wading in with his folks and fixing things that need fixing. He's the first to move off the dime if there is a blockage in the way. He never seems to lose sight of that. And he keeps calling others back to it. But he can't hold that important mindset along with the mindset of being collegial and respectful. For him, a crisis trips a mindset that it's OK to scream at folks.

His colleague is unfailing polite, and never screams at his folks. Yet when faced with a directive from a boss, no matter how nonsensical, his old habitual response is likely to be "Yes, boss." Even when his other, newer leadership mindset knows better.

43. Let go of the idea that "they" are causing your problems, whoever they are.

Ask yourself, "**How is my mindset contributing to these difficulties?**" What is an alternative mind-set, or just a quarter-turn of this mindset, that would allow a breakthrough? I think about that shift as a quarter turn of thinking that allows the light to enter straight to the center of dilemma, a quarter turn of mindset that would cause me to process information differently.

44. Let go of your hold on yes/no, right/wrong, good/bad solutions and responses.

Practice framing questions like this: "To what extent. . . under what conditions? How can I increase the probabilities that...?"

Therefore?

So what do I do about all this? I'm embarrassed to say none of this is new. It's quite different from what we have understood in the recent past, but maybe it's a return to

∞

something old and a discovery of something new, all at once. Perhaps it is the wisdom of three thousand years ago, and the lean manufacturing gurus at once. Quite frankly I'm not at all convinced that there is anything new about all this. More likely it is a recalling of some uncommon common sense.

As a leader I am convinced that these alternative mindsets are a path to a more effective result. And I may simply wish to lead in these ways for reasons beyond effectiveness, resting perhaps in values and a personal choice of how I want to live my life. So what do I do? How do I do it? Isn't it just a matter of deciding? Yes and no. Deciding is necessary, but I don't think it's sufficient.

We all have Achilles heels in this stuff. The question is just which one. Which mindset above, or yet another one, is the place we slip up? Our most likely place to get thrown? What hooks us sufficiently on that item that, as a friend of mine says, "We forget our brains and go stupid"? What helps us return to our brains and our hard won wisdom as quickly as possible? And stay there as long as possible?

It's important to remember, too, that a shift in mindset isn't necessarily about stopping doing one thing, and starting an entirely different response. The mindshifts listed above are often about balance, about percentages, about the question, "How often can I operate from the more effective mindset?" "How can I increase the percentages of that mindset driving my actions, and of that mindset driving the actions of other? How do I do that?"

Let me give an example of a real live organizational case in progress: A colleague and I work with a manufacturing plant that has decided to take its destiny in its own hands; the leadership is increasingly clear that only those in the plant hold the plant's interest and destiny most unquestionably in their hands. While the plant is part of a large corporation and will likely remain so, and must operate within that framework, the plant leadership

∞

team must think like business owners if the plant is to survive
and thrive. And they are beginning to practice that kind of
thinking. This is a new mindset.

Yet it is hard for them not to slip back into old habits when they
are under pressure. The pressure that seems to most throw them
off balance is any directive from corporate, which seems to turn
them immediately into a set of plant overseers doing the
bidding of corporate, no matter what, rather than the smart
group of entrepreneurs committed to doing what is necessary to
the short-term and long-term health of the plant no matter what.
They have trouble staying in the mindset of the entrepreneurs
which they are becoming. They get it, they get it, they forget it.

While the management leaders struggle with old management
thinking, so does the union leadership, often yanking itself back
to the thinking which made it successful, and now holds it
back—the sure knowledge (mindset) that making common cause
with management about the future of the business is being in
bed with the enemy, that the questions of markets and the
future of the business is the business of management leadership
not union leadership.

In the face of these old and very powerful mindsets, the union
and management leadership team has decided that making the
transition to a more flexible, lean production process is the fastest,
best path to business success and the need is urgent. They have
decided to think a different way about production. For several
years they have been engaged in a process to do just that, but it
has been laborious, a company-wide training and roll-out effort.
Now they are all seeing that they need to streamline that process,
to get faster results. And that, they know, requires that they think
in a different way about leadership. The decision is made to move
in a new direction—both of production and leadership. Simple.
Yes? No.

∞

The old habits of leadership, remember, are to take orders from above the plant and respond to the need to roll out corporate initiatives. So their lived leadership experience has been in relationship to those orders and initiatives. Whether the response to those orders is "Yes, boss" and we drop everything else to be best in class at complying (including dropping what we think matters to the future of the plant) or "Yes, boss" and we practice only sufficient compliance, it is the orders from outside that determine what we do, and dominate us, that grab our attention from whatever we were thinking. There is no customer more important than the customer that is our boss. Whether our response is compliant or oppositional, it is a response that is connected to the directive from above and outside, not connected to our own train of thought.

The alternative response is driven by the mindset that as a leadership team we have a train of thought about where this plant needs to go, and we carefully evaluate each "incoming" for the way it can help us take the plant there. That mindset, a mindset of stewardship in a complex system, might produce actions that look similar to the action above, but those actions come from a different place, and have a more focused, stable and flexible trajectory. There is less of a careening from one thing to another, and more of a sense of center and focus.

The group decides it will move forward with its plans for streamlining production its way. Great. Within weeks, the next edict from above is to implement "lean" manufacturing. "Hire this consultant. Do what he says. Fast." The old mindset reasserts itself. The automatic, reflexive question is "Do we do it or not? How do we do it? Can we do it best so we beat out the other plants and look like a winner? What if we can't do it? Will we take a beating?"

An entirely different question from an alternative mindset might be "How could this idea help us achieve what we've said we need

∞

to achieve as a plant? How can it give us a boost in the direction we need to go?"

Meeting after meeting is held in which two mindsets are at war with each other. Among folks. Even within individual heads. Folks are all over the map.

Finally the train of thought takes hold: This idea of lean experiments brings with it resources and push, and we can use this to make the next breakthrough in our production system, to become truly profitable, and to draw in new business. On track. You can feel the energy in the room. The gears engaging. That energy lasts about an hour, until somebody drops the bombshell that corporate (a different place than the lean directive) has ruled that nobody can hire outside help without the sign-off of the CFO of the corporation. The energy flows out of folks through their feet and their seats. Silence. Inaction. Waiting.

The next week the union and management teams go to a conference together. Here's a good opportunity to remind themselves of the train of thought of changes in the markets that require changes in the business. Hopeful sign. Nope. The union on its old track, convinces management that it will not support this "new idea of lean" since it has been unable to see that it is at the heart of the idea it has already committed to called the "company's new production system." Management, with the mindset that change is always resisted has of course rammed the change down their throats. Now management stops dead in its tracks and rescinds the order to "do lean" until things can be sorted out.

The plant leader says, "We can't do this until corporate settles things." Translate "Old mindset has got us in its grip again." New mindset would say, "Well, looks like we can't rely on corporate push and support right now, but until things get

∞

sorted out lets move ahead as best we can on what we ourselves are trying to do."

Is this leadership hopelessly out of step with its own thinking? Have they lost their minds? Are they stupid? Slow? Fearful? Absolutely not. These are smart, dedicated folks trying to do a tough job well. Yet they are living with a common Achilles heel. They have a human tendency to get sidetracked by an old mindset, and every time corporate strikes with a new idea, they snap back into old thinking about what to do. Their story is still in progress, with these choice-points for exercising a new mindset appearing almost daily. Some days the results are pretty good and other days not so good. A human business.

Theirs is, however, an important story. It reminds us that the question for any leader is not "Will I lose my grip on the more effective mindset, on what I say I believe?" But rather "What conditions so challenge me that I lose my grip? And when that happens, and I do lose it, how quickly can I recall my frame of thinking, my train of thought, and what help do I need to do so?"

All of us lose it from time to time, individually and collectively — different circumstances throw different of us. That's why a leadership team with an articulated spoken train of thought carefully considered, written down, and regularly spoken out loud on an ongoing basis, has a better chance of staying on track, because when one person, even the boss loses it, others can call them back on track. And when the norms make it clear that by calling each other back to the train of thought, we are providing important support, then folks don't hang back from speaking truth in such situations, or waiting in embarrassed silence until the boss gets his feet on the ground again.

It has become clear to me that the derailing is not just the function of the wisdom, strength and logic of the plan, of the intelligence of the business case. It is additionally the result of

∞

the power of these more foundational mindsets that can function like unexpected, unseen track switches, throwing our thinking unexpectedly off the main track into a spur in the puckerbrush. Perhaps that's the reason that folks make commitments and break them, that they shape sensible plans and do nothing about them, that they take two steps forward and one back. So, how then do we help them and ourselves in such circumstances?

Here are some protocols and practices that help individuals and groups adopt these mindsets, and stay on track with a more productive train of thought:

- Identify crucial intersections, and make clear the old (don't go there) path as well as the new (go there even if it feels uncomfortable) path.

- Identify the "no matter whats" in each piece of work.

- When you are thrown by some development, describe "the data I see, and the story I tell myself." The story surfaces the mindset, so we can tell alternative stories and practice different mindsets. And we get more skilled at noticing the difference between the data and the story.

- Use the Rule of Six, a Native American thinking discipline that I learned from my friend Paula Underwood. It requires that when we are faced with something we are trying to sort out or understand, we are required to think of at least six possible explanations or understandings. And then where the Western mind would decide which is "right," the native discipline is to hold all six at once.

- Establish specific norms and check fidelity to them.

∞

Whether the stated norms are for a single meeting, or for guiding the ongoing work of a team, they hold us to a certain center. They needn't be many. One powerful one that I have learned recently from colleagues: "Loyalty to those not present."

- Develop the discipline of maintaining a train of thought collectively, writing it down, and checking all "new ideas," directives, and instincts to act fast against it.

- Practice the skills of dialogue: Increase your awareness of the shifts of thinking that occur as you are learning. "When I came into this conversation, I thought. . . and now my thinking has shifted . . . . " It helps one become conscious of shifts of thinking and for a group to share that consciousness.

Good Samaritan

The Good Samaritan
Isn't just about
Someone dying
By the roadside.
It's about
Someone lost
In a hallway
In your organization,
And,
Too busy to pause,
You do.

∞

Life's not a Battle

Life's
Not a battle,
But adventure,
Not a test,
But an
Experiment
We undertake
With curiosity
Because
We want
To know
How something
Works.
'Tis knowing this
As simple fact
Makes all
The difference.

∞

Paths to Transforming Change:
Guidance for Transformational Leaders

- Keep your eye on the prize. What is the vision that stays in your line of sight, no matter what? What values guide you?

- Plan and learn simultaneously.

- Nurture what you want. Tend small plants. Encourage, don't discourage.

- Tend the commons. Make them evident. Care for them together so folks don't get lost in their individual foxholes.

- Go where there is life. Don't move unnecessary boulders up unnecessary hills. Notice where the energy is and move with it.

- Be willing to move slowly at times.

- Encourage talk up and down the line. Conversation transforms.

- Create rich, diverse intersections among people of different mind-sets.

- Give simple, clear, unambiguous signals of direction.

- Set a norm of "all leading, all hands on deck." Share leadership.

- Encourage truth telling. Appreciate people for telling the truth of what they see, for sharing their perspective.

∞

- Invite others into your dilemmas.

- Create new structures to hold new reality. Don't try to make change stick by sheer force of will and personality.

- Focus on people. Know your folks and their strengths and weaknesses in change. Keep your eye on the rear-view mirror to make sure everyone is there.

- Expect to encounter a desert or swamp from time to time. The neutral zone. Wetlands. Expect disorientation with new roles and new context. Use those times for creativity.

- Build in time for rest, recovery, celebration, restoration.

A reservoir within

Each of us needs
A reservoir within,
Because life doesn't happen
On an average.
It has its hurricanes
And droughts,
And lovely days.
So also joy.
So also deep despair.

∞

Some Reflective Questions for Leading Change

Here are some questions that I have found helpful in leading change and living with change in my own personal and professional life:

What is your personal change footprint? We each have a "change footprint" which is our own unique way to move creatively through change. Sometimes we aren't aware of it. Learning more about it, reflecting on it and using it intentionally can be very helpful. When have you navigated a change and the results turned out well? How did you do that? What did you do and how did others help?

What matters most? Our successful navigating of change is dependent on our ability to remember at all times what matters most—our vision, personal and organizational; our values, personal and organizational; the long view of things recalled amidst the demands of the present moment; our commitment at the start of the day of how we want to approach things, no matter what. What will be your individual and collective way to keep your eye on what matters most?

How is change a learning process? As we go through change, we learn, we change our minds. When we think about what lies ahead of us as a time to learn, to experiment, then we are more likely to enjoy the process and to be able to take in data and experiences that are new to us. Shifting from "knowing" to "learning" helps us handle change wisely. What practices will help you examine carefully your way of thinking about how things are and should be, and to notice shifts in that understanding? How will you be able to take in and work with differences in points of view? How will you keep track of what you are learning, collectively?

∞

How is change linked to creativity? Creativity is at the heart of change. All change is an invitation to a creative process which will create a new arrangement, a new situation, a new role for us. Times of change are a good time to stay in touch with creativity — ours and others. It is our aid. What creative processes (gardening, music, poetry, wood-working, photography, dance, painting) are part of your life (or of your past)? How can you create space for them here and now, as you face change?

How does nature change? The natural world changes all the time, and seems to handle it well. Acorns turn into oaks and grow toward the sky, without even a strategic plan, and certainly without e-mail. Birds migrate. Squirrels race around highways in the canopy of the trees. Paying attention to the natural world and asking what it might teach us about change in our own lives can provide insights. How will you have moments to learn from nature? Once a day ask yourself, "What speaks to me from the natural world and what does it have to say about change?"

What about fears? Change can tap natural human fears — natural fears of uncertainty, incompetence, failure, insufficiency, scarcity, loss. In us, and in others. Be compassionate with yourself and others in the midst of change. Are you able to forgive yourself and others for moments when one or another human fear seems to take center stage?

What about the things we love? Let your passion for what you love, your longing for a better way, and your celebration of the small victories along the way, fuel your efforts toward a better world. It is "seeing" abundance, generosity, giftedness, and possibility, that allows us to be present to our natural fears and still move forward with grace, energy and effectiveness.

∞

What are the capacities in you that change will tap? Change stretches us into our untapped gifts, into capacities in ourselves that have lain dormant. Working with change is like learning a new musical instrument or trying a new sport and getting better and better at it.

How do we handle the uncertainties? Change opens a space of ambiguity and uncertainty, often when we'd prefer certainty and stability. I always feel like I'm in a swamp when I am in the midst of uncertainty. A friend has reminded me it is like a "wetland," a space in our lives that does enormously important work for the planet—and for us. A time of sifting, cleansing, dormancy.

How do we find time to learn, to be creative, to stay connected? If change is all these things, then we need space (within us and among us) in order to navigate it wisely—time for conversation, reflection, sharing information, time to consider. Make sure to create the space that allows the change to grow well and fully. Doing that may seem impossible, since change comes on top of an already full life. Yet we must intentionally create the space to be wise about the changes ahead.

∞

A Day of Transition

This is a day
Of transition
To be savored,
A bridge
Between what is
Now past,
And that to come,
Unknown.

Luminous,
The day rises
To meet us.

∞

Welcoming the Feminine Dimensions of Leadership

Over these writings I bent my head.
Now you are considering them. If you
Turn away I will look up: a bridge
That was there will be gone.
For the rest of your life I will stand here,
Reaching across.
      William Stafford

This writing is an invitation to explore territory that is tough, full of uncertainties, confusions. A friend tells me that when there are no words and still we know we must persist, we are in the presence of the transcendent. That is perfect territory for a poet, for whom words are at the heart of the matter, and yet for whom the act of writing is always, like following the tracks of a small animal in fresh snow, an effort to point toward the elusive, the paradoxical, the transcendent. I ask you to join me in that process.

I am aware, as a leader and as a woman, of how difficult it is to capture in precise words the dimensions of leadership that collect around the notion of the feminine. For I am using the word "feminine" not as relating to a particular gender, but as a quality within us all. And I am using the term "leadership" not as conferred by a particular role, or high position, but as a human capacity and orientation widely available although not always evident. And were that not challenge enough, I am urging that we integrate the feminine dimensions in healthy partnership with the masculine dimensions, within us and around us.

The processes and concepts are elusive. Captured by the eastern notion of the Yin and Yang, yes, but elusive. Wordless.

∞

Still, men and women who struggle to lead in healthy ways tell
me that they recognize in themselves and others the hunger for a
balance of the two orientations in their own lives, their
relationships and their organizations. So to honor their efforts,
and with their encouragement, I have set out to put in place some
trail markers on a path we each travel in our own way. I hope this
writing will serve more as a question than an answer perhaps, and
as an invitation to explore a question that makes innate sense to
many of us, out of our instinctive hunger for wholeness in our
lives our relationships and our organizations.

Here is the question before us: **How might we more fully invite
and welcome the feminine dimension of leadership in our
organizations, our relationships and our selves?**

My natural way to begin this paper? To think of the lessons of my
life, the stories. To think of colleagues who have helped me
wrestle with this question. To talk with people. To look at poems,
my own and others, that might be instructive. To recall books that
have shifted my thinking. To think of what might be helpful to
others, particularly practical things—processes, principles and
practices. And to invite you into the same process of sorting and
sifting among the threads that are important to you.

I ask myself, "Can I footnote people, friends and colleagues, not
just books and traditional sources? Can I cite my own life
experience, not some other external authority, and ask questions
rather than have answers?" Those are, for me, the natural ways to
engage in this work, and perhaps I am intuitively reaching toward
some of the feminine dimensions of work, of leadership, which I
am attempting to write about.

Then I find myself asking, "Why should my personal story, my
experience of this discernment matter? Why should yours count
either? You can't footnote experience. You can't cite people's
lives and their impact on us."

∞

Or can we? That is the question that the feminine dimension of leadership poses for all of us. How do we know? What are the many ways? How do we lead? Can we take to heart the Quaker adage, "Let your life speak"?

Now I shift from an internal dialogue to the article at hand.

I used to wonder what the differences were between women as leaders and men as leaders. I wanted to believe that there would be definitive and perceivable differences between the leadership of men and the leadership of women. I no longer think there are. I still have moments when I wish there were, but I haven't seen those differences, and research doesn't seem to have uncovered them.

One can look at one or another woman leader and notice how she leads differently from one or another male leader. I think of Mary Robinson who, as head of state in Ireland, understanding the power of symbol, put the light in the window. But one can also notice women leaders who lead in ways that we would consider more masculine. And one can observe that men show a similar broad range of leadership approaches.

Our observation is complicated by the fact that our minds slip from the word feminine (which embraces a collection of qualities which we all possess to some extent), to the word female (the gender). Like a car that keeps slipping out of gear, we slide from the qualities to the gender. From "feminine" to "female." The two are not the same. Language fails us.

Yet many of us have a sense that the feminine dimensions of leadership–the more personal and inner, the more diffuse, the more creative and artistic, the more holistic and nature-centered, the more inclusive and welcoming—have often been silenced by organizational work processes, structures and norms.

∞

Carol Frenier in her book, *Business and the Feminine Principle*
defines the feminine dimension in terms of four primary
attributes: 1) diffuse awareness 2) a feel for the quick of the
moment 3) acceptance of the cycles of life 4) a feel for deep
community. Other researchers and theorists have strengthened
my awareness of the feminine and masculine, and the need for
each to value the other: Henry Mintzberg's *Crafting Strategy* a
classic HBR piece on strategy as a process that involves both art
and logic; Deborah Tannen's ground breaking work on
communication dynamics between men and women; Carol
Gilligan's classic *In a Different Voice* that reframed ethical
dilemmas to include the voice and perspective of women; Carol
Pearson's *The Hero Within* which helps us understand that all the
classic stories of human development have both feminine and
masculine dimensions, and Irini Rockwell's recent book on the
honoring of the masculine and feminine in the Buddhist
understanding of human relationships.

Still one can cite specific ways that some organizations seem to
inadvertently dampen and discourage the feminine dimension (in
men as well as women). As a result those organizations end up
both dismissive of, and starved for, the missing feminine energies
in their organizational life. Sometimes they swing from one
extreme to another—first convinced that the "soft stuff" is what
they need, and then convinced that the "bottom line" is all that
matters. The lack of integration, respect, steadiness and balance
saps the energy of both men and women. Women are often
singularly saddled with the hard emotional work of the
organization, and with other feminine work such as community
building, aesthetics—if those dimensions get attended to at all.
And of course, as people realize that only part of them is welcome
in organizational life, men as well as women cease to welcome
that other dimension within themselves. Thus, increasingly the
organization is in danger of being blind-sided by realities that are
related to the feminine, including cultural dynamics, emotional

∞

dynamics, creative potential and aesthetic dimensions. This is a world with which most of us have painful first-hand experience.

By the same token, as you may be thinking, in work cultures that are historically feminine it may be necessary to explicitly invite the masculine dimension into the leadership of everyone, so the few men don't have to carry it alone. That necessity of re-balancing has become clearer to me in my work in large urban libraries, where the culture is traditionally more feminine.

If leaders want to tap and focus human energies and talents, they must model and create welcome for diverse gifts and perspectives, including the energies of the masculine and feminine. And if we are to have essential balance and integration of the feminine and the masculine, we need to make sure the feminine (in men and in women) is as welcome and invited into organizational life and into the work of leadership as is the masculine. And that there is real integration of the two within us and around us.

If that work were easy, I doubt that writing this paper would have stirred up as much dialogue around me and within me as it has. As a fairly driven executive for many years, and as a poet, I continue to seek ways to hold onto my own commitment for integration, balance and the presence of both the masculine and feminine in my own life, as well as in the life of the organizations with which I work.

As I facilitate dialogues and design learning experiences with organizations, I learn much about that integration. And I am able to collect, practice and share some notions that seem to entice the feminine energies back into our organizational lives and to help those feminine energies become rooted, particularly within institutions that have evolved in a more masculine field — for example manufacturing, universities, science and engineering-based firms, even symphonies. Such processes are not unfamiliar

∞

to us: they include story telling, community building, inquiry and listening, creative practices like music, poetry, drama or art, and forms of dialogue. Such processes place a high value on participation and inclusion, and elicit more presence than presenting, more listening than lobbying, more creating than constructing, more discovery than direction.

While the challenge of carving out welcoming space for feminine energies in masculine cultures has been at the heart of my work as I have moved among institutions of all kinds, it has not occurred to me to frame what I do in that way. It is more natural for me to speak of the challenge of creating welcome for all perspectives, all voices, all gifts, all kinds of knowledge and experience. And particularly creating welcome for the voices oft silenced. Yet I remain aware that often those silenced are voices (be they male or female) speaking from the feminine orientation.

While more feminine processes are often seen at first glance as "soft," many of them are solid as the mountains and have demonstrated their power over centuries. Some derive, at least in part, from traditional and aboriginal societies. For example, I remain indebted to my Native American colleague Paula Underwood Spencer whose book *Who Speaks for Wolf* provides the business logic for inclusion, and whose practice of the *Rule of Six* teaches us the use of story and scenario to help us break out of whatever thinking box we're in. Some processes come from long spiritual tradition. For example the questioning process utilized in the Courage To Teach programs of Parker Palmer, is derived from a 300-year old Quaker process.

Oddly many of these same traditional processes and patterns are paralleled by the contemporary work of organizational theorists who have designed practices like Appreciative Inquiry, Open Space Technology, World Café. The research support for such approaches is laid out most compellingly for me, in the work of Marcial Losada, Deborah Tannen and Robert Ginnett among

∞

others. So we might say that science and tradition seem to be taking us in similar directions—toward the active and intentional inclusion of what's often been missing: the feminine dimension in leadership.

Still in today's results oriented, bottom-line focused organization, these more feminine practices are often experienced as soft and counter-cultural–even when they have proved to clearly impact the financial bottom line, and even when they are promoted by the men and women leading the organization. It is as if we are seized by the anxiety that is provoked by their being different from the intentional, focused, linear and logical organizational processes, which are more usual, if not satisfying processes. And that anxiety prompts our retreat from the presence of the feminine into the familiar arms of a narrower logic and bottom line–not realizing that the very orientation from which we retreat may well be the path that will serve a fuller logic and a richer bottom line.

Whether introduced by men or women, feminine approaches often run into to the cultural norms of the "traditional" leadership model as well as the more masculine energies that had been running the show. But that doesn't mean they are at odds with individual male leaders, certainly not some of the ones I've worked with. I see men joining with their women colleagues in the discovery, recovery, articulation and introduction of feminine leadership processes, and in important instances, living them into being. For example, I think of....

- Michael Jones and I, at the invitation of the School of Engineering at the University of Michigan at Dearborn, facilitating an engineering-focused conference on systems learning, using music and poetry to link workshops and keynotes designed to stimulate different ways of thinking. By the end of three days of this way of working together, in a world of round tables, engineers with whom I'd worked for years in the auto plants, began to hand me

∞

folded slips of paper. "Here," one or another would say, "It's a poem I wrote." Secret notes from secret poets.

- My physician-leader colleague, Brian Campion, collaborating on the design of a session on dialogue, noting that somehow in a day of our walking around my neighborhood and talking, telling each other important stories of how we ended up where we were, and asking each other questions, he'd found himself being wiser than he thought he could be. He didn't know how it had happened, he said, but he wanted to know how to create that result.

- Tense union-management dynamics that shifted suddenly when one of the young hot-shot big eight accounting firm consultants talked openly and with evident emotion about his critically ill newborn son, and a crusty senior union leader whose wife had been critically ill for a long time, generously offered the younger man encouragement and hope.

- An executive who told me how he finally helped folks move beyond their grief at having to close the founding unit of their fortune 500 firm. "It was a 'buggy whip' story," he said, "And no jobs were lost. Nobody disagreed with the action, and yet nobody could move on. We were stuck. So I did the only thing a thinking engineer could do: I ordered a casket and had it, and flowers, placed in the lobby of the corporate headquarters, and we had a funeral for the old business, and folks who'd been part of that business unit came, and we sang songs, and people cried, and we buried that sucker. And then we could get on with our work."

∞

One can see in each of these experiences, the intuitive introduction of, or the unexpected emergence of, a feminine dimension of leadership. How do we sketch a full range of such qualities? And how do we more intentionally invite them into our leadership work?

The most straightforward way for me to sketch the range of qualities that point toward the feminine orientation in leadership is to lay out word pairs, the first of which points toward the feminine, the second of which points to the masculine. Remember the idea of trail-signs, however: these are not the territory, they are just words to point us toward the territory. These are not meant to be definitive, nor exhaustive, but rather suggestive of the differences that we are pointing toward. And if our minds would let us think that way, we would hold them as dimensions not at odds with each other, but necessary to one another, and resident within each of us. But our minds have minds of their own....

Toward the Feminine	Toward the Masculine
Welcome	Boundaries
Partnership	Competition
Inquiry	Advocacy
Ritual	Rigor
Curiosity	Certainty
Wondering	Knowing
Appreciating	Judging
Accepting	Asserting
Listening	Talking
Nurturing	Challenging
Stories	Analysis
Humanities	Sciences

∞

Appreciating	Challenging
Inviting	Limiting
Empathy	Objectivity
Poetry	Analysis
Music	Words
Art	Science
Creating	Building
Space	Material
Spirit	Object
Sketching	Stating
Exploring	Evaluating
Opening	Choosing
Accepting	Insisting
Emergence	Strategy
Attention	Intention
Caring	Risking

Toward the Feminine   **Toward the Masculine**

I have always thought of the feminine and masculine, and these word pairs, as dancing with each other, as if each word in a pair above is in a continual dance with the other word, in a dynamic relationship that is changing and in which the two are always connected. The symbol of the yin and yang approximate that relationship, suggesting a curved delineation of a difference in which each holds space for the other, in which each rests in the other.

Yet the balanced, respectful dance between masculine and feminine is not easy to hold in organizational life. At least in our culture. We get the idea of the integration, the balance. And then we forget it. Work cultures schooled in one (the masculine, for instance) but unconsciously yearning for the other (the feminine) may swing between them, rather than center in a way that holds both. It seems human at times to want to choose one as better, or

∞

blame one as worse. Or in an enthusiasm for one, to drive out all vestige of the other.   And even those of us who think we understand the dimensions and the balance, may often lose our grip on our understanding of balance and respect and need to be reminded by our colleagues or by life.

It seems to me that leadership work is about just that—holding both sides, and valuing both sides. It is, for instance, about being a precise, disciplined and curious scientist and an aware and gifted story-teller. It is about all the pairs of words above, and in each case not setting down one for the other, but rather recognizing it takes both habits of mind and both disciplines of spirit to find our path forward as individuals, institutions and communities. Like a parent of twins, we hold both at once. We honor the masculine and feminine, within us and around us, and in doing so help the organizations and causes for which we care, to find a healthy path. The feminine is needed not because it trumps the masculine, but because it has been missing from the necessary partnership of the two leadership dimensions.

As each of us looks at the list of word pairs, above, or creates lists of our own making, other stories may well float to mind, stories of when we have tried to choose one side over the other, and life has reminded us of the necessity for both.   It is then, I think, that we are moved to adopt a commitment to inviting the presence of both the masculine and feminine into organizational life, and to welcome the feminine, as the oft under represented dimension, whenever it shows up, and to encourage, nurture and amplify it.

In my own life, I had the concept of balance, but living the balance was never easy. Again and again, I could feel myself pulled into the competitive dynamics that exercised one dimension of my gifts, and silenced the other. Being nominated for the White House Fellows program was one such pull: convinced in my heart of hearts that I was not White House Fellow material, I nonetheless figured I could learn something useful by going

∞

through the selection process. So I plowed ahead. I cleared one hurdle (surprisingly) after another, until I was in the final 32 from which 15 Fellows would be selected for a year's assignment as assistant to a US cabinet secretary or the President.

In midst of this competitive hurdle-jumping, my phone rang one day. The caller introduced himself saying that he worked at the Pentagon and he had noticed that I was among the White House Fellow finalists. He explained his reason for calling: "I went through the selection process a few years back. I had no idea what to expect, and I found it fairly unsettling. So I'm calling to say that if you want to talk through the process, or do some practice questions, or if there is anything I can do to help, please give me a call. Here's my number."

I took down the man's name and his number. We talked for a little while that day, and I never felt the need to call him back. Yet I was profoundly encouraged by the generosity and welcome from this stranger.

I was aware that what he did that day (his gentle, generous reaching out from the Pentagon, his welcome to me, his offer of help) was a kind of feminine leadership. I kept his name and number, and later when I became a White House Fellow, the name on that scribbled slip of paper meant more to me: Colin Powell. Powell's generous call came long before he was head of the Joint Chiefs of Staff, or United States Secretary of State, the position from which he has most recently retired. I keep that phone call in mind to stay clear in my own understanding that this kind of energy or approach, transcends gender, career role, and background.

How then do we create conditions where both the feminine and the masculine perspectives are invited, valued, celebrated, and heard? In organizations where the feminine dimension has been historically less visible, less openly articulated and less

∞

appreciated than the masculine, how do we create conditions for it to be more fully present? What guidance can we offer ourselves?

First I think we do well to turn to each other, to pay attention to our own experiences, and to learn from those communities of practice that inform our work in organizations. Increasing our own awareness of the practices, processes and guidance that shift the balance in a healthy way, is an important step. And sharing what we are learning in that process is key.

Thus, I include below some of my own collection of practices, processes and guidance, and invite you to similarly share yours.

Guidance about processes:

There are many work processes in which the feminine dimension is deeply imbedded. Some are very familiar, although we might not think of them in this context. Using these processes increases the presence of the feminine dimension of leadership in the organization. And the disciplined and regular use of these structures helps those feminine dimensions take root. Here are some on which I rely:

- **Check-in and Check out**. This simple process for beginning and ending work creates space for all voices, and invites all manner of contribution. Thus it sets, by example, important norms of inclusion and openness.
- **Dialogue**. Dialogue creates a communication space for listening deeply and for becoming increasingly aware of ones own thinking as well as the perspectives of others.
- **Open Space Processes**. There are many variants on these deeply democratic processes for shaping common purpose, work and strategy collectively.

∞

A good starting place is the work of Harrison Owen.

- **Creative Processes.** Non-verbal processes involving art forms of various kinds help people shift out of words and into other forms of knowing. There are many processes that provide simple introductions into the world of the arts. Useful starting places include the work of Julia Cameron, Frederik Franck, Michael Jones' book, *Creating an Imaginative Life.* and Michael Gelb.

- **Appreciative Inquiry.** This process helps us balance our trained tendency to problem-solve, with the ability to spot what is going well and amplify it. The process also brings to a conscious level that which is the deepest positive motivation within people. David Cooperrider is the innovator who created this process.

- **World Café.** This process allows any number of folks to develop intimate and focused conversations around an important topic, in a process that can quite quickly create visible threads of shared understanding. See Juanita Brown's book on the subject.

- **Clearness Committee**. This process for exploring a dilemma creates exceptionally safe space in which a person can come to greater clarity by responding to completely open questions posed by a small group of people over a period of three hours. Parker Palmer details that process as part of his work in *The Courage to Teach.*

- **Story Telling.** Perhaps the source of this would be the human tradition around fires, for millennia. Invite story by asking genuinely curious questions, and letting story unfold.

- **Scenario Work.** Scenario telling is the process of creating alternative stories of the future (or the

∞

past) and rather than trying to figure out which one is true, holding all of them, and watching the unfolding events. It increases our ability to take in all kinds of data. The contemporary form of this is sketched in Peter Schwartz' *The Art of the Long View* and the timeless form is represented in Paula Underwood's *Rule of Six*.

Guidance about principles:

Here are some principles which help me create more balanced spaces–spaces in which the feminine is invited, cherished and celebrated, along with the masculine:

- Pay close attention to the implicit messages of space and design. Use circles, natural light, color, living plants, and beauty of all kinds. Once the leader begins to pay attention to these dimensions, others seem to follow suit. Recently, before we began a planning retreat, a local police chief was rearranging work tables in more of a circle because, as he told me, "It's too squared off and we can't see each other." We laughingly reminded each other that all good work begins with rearranging furniture.

- Balance advocacy with inquiry. Marcial Losada's research on successful leadership teams reminds us that those teams balance their communication 50/50 between advocacy and inquiry. The teams that are in the tank tend to be closer to 80/20 in favor of advocacy.

- Notice what upsets you about the leadership approach of others and explore how that voice or approach is accepted or denied by you within you. Pay attention to the balance of the feminine and masculine within you.

∞

- In framing every dilemma, make sure that both the male energies and the female energies are honored and balanced. In your response as a leader, and in all the other design dimensions of your organization, watch carefully and ask others to be on the watch for dynamics that subtly drive out the feminine perspective. Invite both the masculine and feminine, and seek a "third" way whenever folks are tempted to chose one way over the other.

- Intentionally set organizational norms that invite and hold both male and female leadership dimensions. I am drawn to threesomes of norms (perhaps the threesome naturally holds masculine, feminine and the third way, all at once). Here are my favorite examples–

  - From the work of the Courage to Teach community the threesome of creating space that is bounded, charged, welcoming.
  - From Buddhist practice the three energies of fierceness, tenderness and playfulness.
  - From the norms of a middle-school community in which the students naturally took off muddy shoes after a rainy-day fire drill: Take care of yourself, take care of each other, take care of this place.
  - From the computer simulation of birds flocking, rules that create conditions for random dots on a computer screen to flock, naturally as birds do: don't get too close to the next bird, go about the same speed as every body else, sort of fly toward the center of the flock.

Guidance about personal practices:

It is increasingly evident that welcoming both feminine and masculine is about more than just the external world–it is also about the world within each of us, where the masculine and

∞

feminine create their own relationship. I have come to realize that I need inner practices that help me hold that understanding. It has become increasingly clear to me that if the presence of those capacities, orientations, or differences within me are not accepted and cherished there, it is unlikely that I can usefully participate in creating a workable integration, a creative relationship of the masculine and feminine energies in the external world, in the world of organizations.

That realization has pointed me toward several personal practices that are increasingly important to me including time in silence, listening, meditation, journaling, arts of all kinds, and being in nature. I realize that each of us has our own personal approaches to creating balance from within. My purpose in sharing my list is only to suggest the value of each of us attending to such practice in a way uniquely suited to who we are as a human being.

Leaders create conditions that are either enlivening or deadening. Like architects or designers we create space—emotional space, thinking space, working space. Our ability to serve depends on how well that space frees the resources around us, including the energies of the feminine and masculine dimensions of leadership within us, and around us.

∞

Competitor

You have
No possible
Competitor in being
Wholly who you are.
In such
A race
As that,
The field
Is completely
Yours.

∞

Research Logic for Dialogue

As we practice the skills of dialogue, it is helpful to keep in mind some of the research findings about the power of dialogue in organizational work, and the contribution dialogue can make to the high performance of leadership teams.

I would point you toward the work of three leadership theorists and their research: First, Ron Heifetz in *Leadership without Easy Answers* underlines the power and importance of a leader creating a holding environment for people in order for them to come to new understandings of how to respond to novel and daunting challenges. One definition of dialogue would be that it is a conversational holding environment for sustained thinking together about important challenges.

The second is the work of Daniel Goleman, first in *Emotional Intelligence* (an idea that once was novel and now is a standard way of thinking in our society) and most recently in *Primal Leadership* (a shorter version of which is in the March-April 2000 HBR article "Leadership that Gets Results"). Goleman highlights the positive relationship between the skills of emotional intelligence --- self awareness, self management, social awareness and social skill --- and leadership effectiveness. Those skills are central for dialogue as well. In addition, he distinguishes six styles of leadership, and considers their impact on the climate of the organization. His research indicates that those styles that have the highest positive correlation with favorable climate in an organization are based on emotional intelligence skills (visionary, affilliative, democratic, and coaching), whereas pacesetting has the least effect on positive climate, and a coercive style has a negative one.

∞

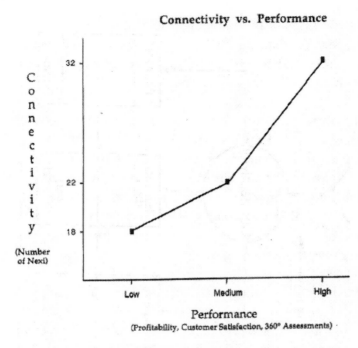

Connectivity vs. Performance

Connectivity
(Number of Nexi)

32

22

18

Low   Medium   High

Performance
(Profitability, Customer Satisfaction, 360° Assessments)

The third provides the clearest logic for learning and practicing dialogue, particularly in the leadership team's strategy work. It is found in the research of Marcial Losada, a

©2000 Meta Learning • 2280 Georgetown Blvd., Ann Arbor, MI 48105 • mlosada@earthlink.net

mathematical psychologist, whose model and research provide a systems understanding of the impact of dialogue on key organizational results. Losada's team of researchers collected data on thousands of hours of strategic conversation involving leadership teams. Rigorous analysis of that data proved that the strongest business results (measured in dollars of profit, in customer satisfaction statistics, and in worker satisfaction statistics) correlated strongly with a quality of conversation marked by a high connectedness or mutual influence among the leaders (the term he uses is "nexi"), and that the components of that connectedness or influence were a 6/1 ratio between positivity and negativity, a 50/50 ratio of advocacy to inquiry, and a 50/50 ratio between focus on the internal capacities (personal as well as organizational) and the external context (outside the individual and outside the organization).

∞

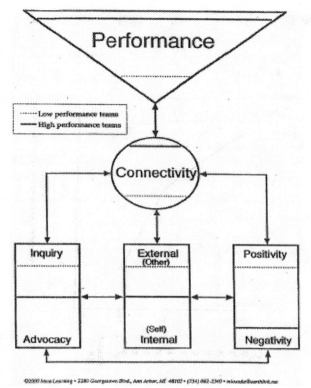

If you look at Losada's model (his more detailed research findings are arrayed as Lorenz attractors in which the effective teams show the classic butterfly pattern of the Lorenz attractor and the least effective teams practice conversations that devolve into a single point attractor, a perfect representation of the kind of pointless stuck conversations that all of us have been party to one time or another) you see that the place to begin is with the 6/1 positivity to negativity. It is the gate. But the 50/50 balance overall in the conversation between advocacy and inquiry, along with the balance of internal and external are equally important to success, and all these dimensions together create a dynamic in which leaders influence and are open to influence, in which they are able to learn their way through challenging and novel developments.

∞

Applewood

Apple wood is what I need,
Gnarled apples wood,
Old, beyond growing apples, and not straight
As woodcutters would like,
But limbs of apple trees,
Twisted and perfect for a fire.

A fire builder's view of wood
Is different from the view
Of those who cut and split and stack.

I love the odd shaped ones,
Unlike each other,
Small ones, each unique,
A story in themselves,
So when they're placed upon the fire
They leave a natural space
One to the next,
Because they're crooked,
And not even, not alike.

It's in those spaces grows the fire,
With easy sparking,
Without tending.

I need to tell him
that the big straight logs,
green wood, will never do.

Give me dry apple wood
From broken, fallen trees.
It's best for fires.

∞

Dialogue: A Short Primer

A working definition of dialogue: Dialogue is a quality of conversation, of speaking and listening, that can create greater understanding within us and among us.

Practices that open space for dialogue:

- **Take time to rearrange the furniture.** Over the years as I have worked with colleagues, leaders and groups to create space for high quality conversation, I've come to trust that before we begin our conversation, and often even before anyone else enters the room, I must take the time to rearrange the furniture in a way that encourages warm, open, honest communication. Rearranging chairs, and tables, getting rid of lecterns, raising window shades to bring in natural light, adding natural flowers and plants— all create an alive and welcoming space for conversation. My simple rule: all good work begins with rearranging the furniture—not only the physical furniture, as it turns out, but the fixed furniture of our minds, the tight edgy ways of thinking that keep us from opening out to others.

- **Shift from lines and squares to circles and arcs.** In the arrangement of furniture, as well as in the language we use, this change from the world of linearity to the world of circles and curves, allows us to relax, to see each other, to gather around the fire of our conversation. The practical matter of setting the conversational "table" so that it is beautiful and inviting, is critical if the initial conditions that people see when they enter are to guide them toward the quality of conversation we seek.

- **Shift from knowing to wondering.** Dialogue is a safe place for wondering, uncertainty and confusion. Allow

∞

yourself to shift onto unfamiliar and uncertain ground, to
wonder rather than know.

- **Shift from statements to questions.** Sometimes the
  greatest wisdom in dialogue comes when somebody asks a
  powerful and very thought-provoking question, one that
  draws everyone's interest.

- **Shift from certainty to curiosity.** Allow your attention to
  shift from what you know for sure to what you are
  genuinely curious about.

- **Assume welcome; extend welcome.** Dialogue is a
  commons, a public space which belongs to all of us, so
  welcome is assumed by all and extended by all.

- **Practice increasing your awareness of your feelings,
  thoughts and reactions, without judgment or comment.**
  Notice what is going on inside you. Understand that it is
  inside of you. Be with your feelings, thoughts, reactions,
  as if they were weather on a weather map: "Ah, a storm.
  How interesting. Look at that lightening. Ah, now the
  storm passes. A bit of blue sky appears." "Ah, I'm angry
  at what was said. How interesting. Now that passes, and I
  notice I am experiencing pleasure in the conversation."

- **Speak only for yourself, and from your own experience.**
  It's tempting to reflect on someone else's life, or
  observations; it is more useful to bring our own experience
  to the conversation and to allow others to do that as well.
  Speak from the heart and the moment, and from your own
  grounded experience.

- **Speak from the center of the self to the center of the
  circle.** Listen to your inner wisdom and speak from that
  place, not from rehearsed notions, nor abstractions. Rather

∞

try to figure out what is uniquely your voice, your point of view here and now. Simply offer your point of view to the collective, placing it metaphorically in the center of the circle.

- **Turn away from debate.** Sometimes it's tempting to get engaged in a mini-debate, back and forth with someone whose point of view is at odds with yours. Resist that urge to play the usual "tennis game" of back and forth. Simply offer your point of view and let it be. Give up the back and forth game.

- **Listen for your own true voice as if it were a shy animal.** Realizing it may be shy, listen for the fresh, less practiced, in-the-moment voice of your centered self. Notice the feelings that signal that true fresh voice. Your own true voice. Wait for it patiently. Support its expression.

- **Be willing to be raggedy.** The essential voice, in touch with the shy self, may not be practiced, smooth, slick. It may be confused, emotional, embarrassed, in the midst of experiencing and sorting things out. Give it space to be itself in its own way. Honor that in yourself; honor it in others.

- **Think twice before speaking more than once.** You may feel the urge to speak quickly and often. Remember that whenever your voice is in the center, another voice, perhaps a shy voice, is remaining silent. Sometimes saying less is better and speaking slowly is fine.

- **Listen (inside and outside) for information not confirmation.** Set aside judgments of yourself and others. Suspend your assumptions and consider that alternative ones might be as useful. Notice what is surprising to you.

∞

Give up your need to hear what you agree with or what you expect. Listen with interest, curiosity.

- **Allow for silence**. Silence can be productive. It may mean people are thinking, considering, taking in what has been said.

- **Listen generously**. Assume that ideas, observations, stories all come from a desire to somehow contribute. Consider that ideas build upon each other even if you can't see how they hook logically one to the other.

- **Seek and welcome difference**. Remember that difference of opinion can be helpful because it sharpens our collective understanding. Let it be. Without debate and without rushing in to smooth things over.

- **Change your focus**. Move away from conclusions toward observations. Notice what you are noticing and what meaning you are making of it.

- **In the midst of difficulty, turn toward wonder**. When what you are hearing is hard to accept, is difficult for you, try practicing curiosity and compassion toward yourself, and toward the other. Try wondering about why it is so hard.

- **Experiment with giving up the need to speak**. Try just listening for long periods of time. Remember that listening and waiting to speak are not the same thing. Listen without thinking about a response. Listen as an ally, to understand.

- **Speak with your fresh voice**. Resist the need to say what you usually say. Sit in silence until you find yourself

∞

moved to say something that is truly of this moment, in this particular conversation.

- **Bring 100% of yourself and allow for 100% of the other.** Allow for the wisdom of what at first seems irrelevant, in yourself, in others.

- **Bring the gift of your complete attention and presence.** Set aside all distractions, internal and external, and be wholly, completely present to this dialogue, here and now.

The circles of our conversation

The circles of our conversation
Help us face each other
And the task before us,
With a hopefulness
We had not known
Until we met.

∞

Dialogue and Measurement

"How do you know it works?" he asked
Of dialogue. I said I didn't know.
Like asking if a kiss worked
Or if a hug had done its job.

They <u>say</u> it does.
The listening helps, they say.
But then again, how do they know?
What can you measure of a glance?

If you can't measure it, they say,
Forget it.
Here's what I say to you,
Toss out the yardstick,
And let's value what is true.

∞

Dialogue:
Capacities and Stories

As published in "Learning Organizations" Edited by Sarita Chawla and John Renesch Productivity Press April 1995

I have come to view dialogue as a process central to the development of learning organizations. This is a view widely held among those who work with learning organizations and learning communities.

I have also come to view dialogue as a capacity in each of us. That is a much less widely held view. I believe that we may have forgotten our capacity for dialogue as individuals and as organizations, or neglected its development. Thus learning about dialogue is really a matter of rediscovery, of recalling what we have forgotten to remember. This paper is about dialogue understood in that light.

I know no way to convey this understanding of dialogue but to tell a story.

Not long ago, I was working with a group of executives in a retreat. Two days into a session on teamwork this operating group from a Fortune 500 was struggling with the perverse effects on teamwork of an element of its financial incentives package. As only one of the operating units, the group had no power to unilaterally change the corporate policy. The group saw no leverage for getting the corporation to change. It was however clear that the incentive structure made real team effectiveness nearly impossible. This had been frustrating them for a long time, and had become an insurmountable impediment to much that they wanted to accomplish.

∞

I suggested that a struggle like this might be seen as a kind of hologram, containing all the patterns and problems that were interesting and important to the corporation and to their work. And I asked if they would be willing to take a couple of hours and work on this issue in a slightly different way. They were delighted to try something that might loosen the knot that they kept finding themselves entangled in, and a change of pace seemed welcome so they quickly agreed.

I asked if they would follow some simple guidelines for a different kind of conversation: Only one person could speak at a time, and as they spoke they were to hold a small rock (I carry a small polished heart-shaped rock and I fished it out for the occasion). They were to relinquish the rock only when they had completed their thought. They should then pass the rock to someone else who signaled they wished to speak, or place it in the center for someone else to pick up. They were to begin by talking about where they were with this issue, in this moment. They were to "speak from the I and from the moment, and listen from the perspective of the group."

One man took the rock. He spoke with deep passion about how rotten the current policy made him feel, how painful it was for him to explain it to his subordinates, how deeply he wanted to change it. The rock passed from person to person. Sometimes the energy of an idea would cause someone to "piggyback" quickly on the idea before, or to finish someone's sentence, and people would laugh and say "Remember the rock," or "You have to have the rock." The conversation sped up. It slowed down. There were periods of silence. One person took the rock and said, "I am not where I was when we started this conversation. Something really has changed my way of thinking." Bit by bit there emerged an entirely new way of conceiving the problem and shaping possible solutions, until finally, after a long silence, one person said, "I see

∞

how we might work to change this...." and he proposed a very participative and involving process for incubating a new approach, with a clear goal of greater fairness and equity, and volunteered to contribute his own financial gain to the pot to make it work. People began to weave together an approach that would have seemed impossible when they began the conversation. They ended in silence.

I asked if they felt finished and settled with this issue that they had been gnawing at for months and years. They said "yes," perhaps sensing that each of them had a clear idea of the collective goal, and would immediately do whatever could be done to move forward on this work, and that after this conversation there was no way not to do what they had given voice to.

What is dialogue then, as it emerges in this experience?

In a sense, dialogue is not complicated. It is just good conversation, over the back fences of our lives. It is continued, thoughtful exchange about the things that most matter. It is time to sit under the apple tree together and talk, as the ideas and thoughts come to us, without agenda, without time pressures. It is the kind of conversation that we have forgotten in the pace of western, modern life. Or in the language of both Maya Angelou and Paula Underwood Spencer, who speak to us from the African-American and Native American traditions respectively, from cultures that practiced dialogue, it is reminding us of "that which we have forgotten to remember."

The concept of dialogue comes to us from many historical and contemporary sources. One form of it comes out of the Greek tradition of the Socratic dialogue in which the student is led by the master to a greater level of wisdom. Some form of dialogue is found in most traditional pre-industrial and pre-agricultural societies, and is particularly visible in the Native American

∞

culture, where the process acknowledges that it is necessary to "talk and talk until the talk starts."

In contemporary management literature, dialogue figures most prominently in the work of Peter Senge's *The Fifth Discipline*, where it serves as one of the processes central to systems thinking, and finds its intellectual roots in the dialogue work of the physicist David Bohm. Various forms of dialogue are reflected in the work of Bill Isaacs and his colleagues with the MIT Dialogue Project, in the work on organization as community and the concept of work as "nourishment for life" of the "Naerings Liv" project of Juanita Brown and David Isaacs, in the exploration of corporate strategy employed by Diana Smith, and in the work about the nature of learning and inquiry of Parker Palmer. All of us are part of a contemporary dispersed, virtual community exploring the power of dialogue, in a variety of different ways.

For most of us, the pattern of dialogue requires new ways of thinking about and evaluating communication. If we see the goal of communication as to decide something or do something, we are unable to discern the way in which dialogue, without a seeming focus on decision or action, enables individuals to focus their personal energies almost unconsciously so that once the dialogue has ended people go forth and act in a remarkable level of concert, without the need for action plans or coordination or checking. Such patterns have been noted in the modes of communicating of Asian and Native American cultures.

Since dialogue taps ways of communicating not often represented in the dominant Western culture, ways that may be more reflective of minority cultures, of marginal cultures, or the cultures less visible in our organizational world, these ways are not going to feel comfortable and familiar, at the start, for leadership elites who have achieved great success, in a certain range of situations, by communicating in modes decidedly un-dialogue-like.

∞

We should note that dialogue is a different and often unfamiliar way of being together in communication, and we should acknowledge that and be prepared for it. If we overlook the unfamiliarity of this mode of communicating, we will also make it unlikely that others can evaluate accurately its value-added in our organizational lives. Instead we will mistakenly evaluate it in traditional modes (of decisions taken by meetings end and measures of closure) and judge it within the time bounds of the meeting, rather than in the longer and more important time frames of future action and alignment.

I am reminded of the many stories of North Americans negotiating with Asians and considering the process of talking and silence without any seeming progress, as pointless and unproductive. The same North Americans have found the level of accord and speed of implementation quite astonishing, in comparison with the level of struggle over implementation in Western cultures. And seldom do they realize the relationship between the slowness of speaking and the ease of acting.

The impossibility of using our usual evaluation, is early apparent. In very powerful dialogues, I have found participants unwilling to evaluate the experience during the session. In one such dialogue, after I had, in good traditional educator form, asked the group to evaluate a pilot experience with dialogue, one usually driven and out-come oriented executive said to me after a long period of collective silence, "I cannot do this. I can't evaluate this. For three days we have engaged in a level of communication and exploration, the likes of which I have not experienced before, and I for one, am not willing to stop the dialogue in order to evaluate it. For three days we have suspended judging and instead we have listened to each other. I'm not going to stop now."

Yet the practice of dialogue is not without its dark side, its seeming dangers for people. We know from heatedly negative reports of "dialogue sessions" that for some people the process is powerful, for others it is "full of sound and fury, signifying nothing." For still others it may open their understanding in ways that are emotionally overwhelming and that the process is not prepared to help them handle. And there may be instances in which as dialogue leaders we are using the intensity of the mode for our own purposes, subtly and in invisible ways manipulating the process to meet our own needs.

So this methodology, because it makes space for people to explore very difficult things, must be handled with great care, very gently, and very ethically. This means that we must, as those designing and leading dialogues, be aware of our own power and of the attractive power of the process, and ensure that it is not coercive. And we must build real safety within the experience.

What purpose does dialogue serve and what capacities does it build in us?

I think of dialogue as seeking to build deeper understanding, new perceptions, new models, new openings, new paths to effective action, and deeper and more enduring, even sustainable, truths. And I believe dialogue has as its purpose, honoring development of individuals and ideas and organizations, at a very deep level. It opens paths to change and clears space for organizational transformation by changing first the inner landscape. We change the world at least in part by changing the way we perceive the world, the way we think about cause and effect, the way we conceptualize the relationships among things, and the meaning we ascribe to events in that external world. Organizational change means changing our internal landscapes as leaders. And I believe that such change is only undertaken by us only when we reach a place in our lives where we want to change those landscapes. It is not something that one or another change-oriented initiative is going to do for us or to us. Such changes in our internal landscape are encouraged by the openness, and reflective and collective process of dialogue. Dialogue opens

∞

pathways for change–within us and among us. And from that opening, comes space for organizational and social change.

Most of the traditional thinking about change is more mechanistic, and shows change as structured and planned, change as engineered and driven into organizations. Interesting how we hold as a simple truth that resistance is a necessary component of managing change. We say that managing change means managing resistance. Perhaps we should note instead that resistance is a natural part of managing change the way we have managed change. It is natural no doubt, when change is managed in instrumental, mechanistic ways. But dialogue builds capacities that dissolve resistance.

What capacity does dialogue build within us?

Dialogue builds capacities, in the same way that exercise builds capacities in the human body, slowly and over time giving us new capacities and strengthening existing capacities. Those capacities may include:

• Listening as an ally, listening for understanding, for the piece of the mosaic that might be missing from our own and the collective understanding, the piece which is key to a decision or to successful implementation.

• Asking questions from a "place of genuine not knowing." Dialogue increases our skills at inquiry.

• Allowing for the time and space to finish a thought. Bringing forth thoughts in real-time that are not finished, that are fresh and passionate and alive.

• Finding value in silence, in time to think, in reflection.

∞

•Granting others the respect of being an authority about their own thoughts and feelings.

•Noticing our own internal responses and learning to co-exist with those responses. We notice what is happening in our response to an idea, without needing to actually respond.

•Building a hospitable, bounded and open place for the consideration of perspectives so that we can build a powerful mosaic of common understanding.

•Learning to be provoked and not close down, to step into the center of the provocation, to consider equally the ideas which provoke us and those that resonate with us.

•Learning to listen deeply without the urge to fix, nor counter, nor argue.

•Noticing the nature of our thinking. We learn to give up blaming and judging others, to become more compassionate with ourselves and others.

•Dialogue helps us to develop the capacity to move into and toward difficult issues in a welcoming fashion because we can notice the difficulty without being "hooked."

We come then to understand dialogue as a way to build mental, spiritual and interpersonal muscle with power in our lives and in our organizations. It builds it, not overnight, but over time and that muscle develops differently in different people.

About that capacity, another story: I recall a dialogue with a CEO and part of his leadership team. We are in the midst of a dialogue on "freeing the human spirit." Originally I had designed this strategic dialogue as being about "quality, diversity and change,"

∞

but the CEO had said that while he realized that such specific topics were more understandable to engineers like himself, the real challenge to the corporation was "freeing the human spirit" and we might as well say it straight out. He was convinced that we had to learn to make it possible for people to come to the work with all the talents, energies and power that were potentially theirs. Now we were in the midst of a three day exploration of how to free the human spirit, and were using excerpts of readings from a broad range of literature (Martin Luther King, Peter Senge, Charles Handy, Paula Underwood, Carol Gilligan and others) to spark our conversation. We were talking about learning, and knowing, and about mental models. The morning's readings began with Plato's *Allegory of a Cave* in which the ancient Greek philosopher describes human beings chained to a wall, looking at shadows cast by figures behind them, figures which because of the chains, they don't know exist. And they see the shadows as the only possible reality. This is the conversation about mental models and how we know what we know, from over two thousand years ago. Tough and serious questions emerge.

"Once we've been out of the chains and realize the nature of reality, what are we required to do?" "We're required to return to the cave..." someone says. "And?" Long silence. "And tell the others what we've learned." "Or to take their hand and lead them out." "But they are still chained." And one executive, a senior woman says, "I don't want your hand. I just want you to listen to me." Stunned silence. What does it mean to listen to those we believe are chained? Who are wrong? Who are not yet enlightened? The question is still on my mind eighteen months later. And on theirs.

Then in a later dialogue, a group of engineers is wrestling with the same reading. I have given them task: "Draw the cave that Plato describes. Do the specs of the cave." A group of men are circled around the flip-chart calling out to the man with the magic marker "No, no, it says right here that there is a wall in the back of the

∞

cave, and so it would have to be this way, so the light comes in at an angle....." Detail by detail they sketch the cave, more and more clearly. As they finish, one engineer says "Well, you could draw it the way we have, or," he says, flipping to a clean sheet of newsprint, and doing a quick sketch, "You could draw it like this." His sketch is of the human brain. There is silence.

Later one of the plant leaders, after a small group dialogue about what Martin Luther King had to say to us in his *Letter from the Birmingham Jail*, and after reflecting about what great gap King would now point to between our vision and the current reality, about what he would require of us, and about what action we should take, the plant leader says, "My life is changed by this letter. How could we ever have seen King as just a trouble-maker? The issues he raises are for all of us, not just for Blacks. I for one am going to take this letter back and read it with my guys in the plant. We all have to read this and talk about what it means for us."

How do we create space for dialogue?
How do we start dialogue and how do we sustain it?

There are many possible prompts or beginning points to dialogue: meditation, quiet, writing, reflective exercises, readings, music, the practice of certain communications techniques. David Bohm suggested that there be no explicit prompts, no formal process yet many of us may find it less daunting to enter a space of dialogue by following some recognizable road signs, or paths.

For me, perhaps because my early training was in literature, I find the written word, particularly carefully excerpted pieces of literature from diverse genres and diverse cultures, an effective prompt to dialogue. People have said to me that because of such readings received and read in advance, they find themselves in a different frame of mind when they arrive at a dialogue, as if they have begun an internal dialogue already, which then becomes

∞

collective and involves the voices of others, when they come together with others around the table. The readings create a reflective space in advance of our coming together. Readings that are classic, or from other cultures, remind us of the seriousness and importance of those issues with which we are struggling, and they remind us that the thoughts of others can be a resource to us in the struggle.

I would suggest, moreover, that whatever the opening to dialogue, it should encourage our examining of our own assumptions, and ways of thinking, and it should also move us to consider different ways of thinking that allow for healthy change.

We might characterize dialogue as a profound openness to the vitality of real diversity. It is a process which produces a collective examination of ideas, a collective sense of participation, and a collective wisdom. It is a collective process in which wisdom emerges not from our finding the appropriate path of thinking like the wise one at the head of the table, but rather from coming to a deeper understanding than any one of us had to begin with.

Dialogue is perhaps born out of a sense of incompleteness, of needing something more, and of being hungry for something that is currently beyond us. It seems to reflect a collective sense of needing to move beyond where we are at the moment, without necessarily having a destination in mind nor a particular problem or crisis that pushes us. It is an inquiry, a questioning, a wanting to move to a more satisfying place, together.

What contributes to dialogue?

Here is my list, to which I encourage your additions, from your experience:

∞

a. Readings sent out in advance, which put people in a different frame of mind. Readings model the image of multiple voices and perspectives, over time and space, and make considering the diverse wisdom within the room less of a leap since we are already considering the wisdom from outside the room. Also effective is individual reflective writing completed quietly as a prelude to dialogue.

b. A program design which focuses on emptying a space for people to fill with reflections, rather than filling an already-crowded space with more concepts.

c. The choice of a setting which is reflective, calm, away from the fray.

d. A round table or round circle to give people a sense of shared leadership and to allow all individuals to see each other more completely, listen more completely and be heard more completely.

e. Communication about the process that puts people in a frame of mind to slow down, back off, listen and reflect. Here we must attend to the introduction of the process in a way that meets people where they are and enables them to settle into the process. It is important not to suggest that dialogue is something that only the initiated can do. We should suggest that dialogue taps a capacity in each of us that can easily come to the surface, given the space in our lives to do so.

It is important to set the stage in quiet ways, ways that value who people are and where they are, and

∞

in ways that open pathways to dialogue. Beginning with some thoughts about the process itself and having individuals do some quiet work on personal perspective-setting is helpful. I often begin with Ira Progoff's steppingstones exercise, asking people to list for their own reflection the steppingstones that have brought them to where they are in their lives as a way to put this present time of their lives in perspective. Sometimes I provide simple written or verbal guidance on dialogue, for each of us to use to reflect on our own contributions to the process. They include:

• Speak from the heart and the moment, and from your own experience; listen from the community, from the collective;

• Listen without thinking about responding;

• Listen for information not confirmation;

• Begin thinking in terms of "I wonder...." or "Where I am on this issue now is...."

• Allow for silence. It may mean people are thinking, considering;

• Suspend assumptions and consider alternative ones that might be just as useful;

∞

• Assume that the ideas and
observations of others come from a
desire to contribute;

• Expect that ideas build upon each
other even if they don't link logically
one to the other;

• Remember that difference of
opinion can be helpful, because it
sharpens our understanding;

• Move away from conclusions and
toward observations; notice what
you are noticing, and what meaning
you are making of it;

• Sometimes in communication, less
is better, and slowly is fine.

With this guidance, I believe we help people rediscover the power
of dialogue, and the capacity for its emergence everywhere in
their lives, and in their organizations.

Let me end with two stories about the capacity in each of us for
dialogue, and the potential for dialogue to emerge anywhere,
everywhere, even in the most unexpected places, when we give it
space to do so.

I was working with a global organization tentatively examining
the potential for becoming a learning organization in order to
increase its effectiveness with its clients. Forty of its young stars,
peppery, hard-charging, talented people from all over the world
had been together for a week. As part of our work on shared-
vision, I had asked them to draw pictures of their individual
visions of us as a learning community. Remarkable pictures

∞

emerged on the sheets of newsprint, to be posted on the walls. One man said, as he was drawing a pattern of little different colored X's to represent the group , "Wow, it's in the shape of a heart." The man beside him said "You stole my idea..." as he too found that his pattern was heart-shaped. We sat in a circle on the floor with our art work taped to the walls as a backdrop and dropped into a deep, quiet space of dialogue, talking quietly and slowly about what we saw in the drawings as we worked on them, and now. Then our dialogue ended and we were back in our seminar room, out of the circle, in the rows of chairs, and one of the men said, "That was a remarkable conversation, but I don't see how it could happen with clients, or with our partners. I don't see how we could do it. It's easy for you," he said of me, "to lead us to such a deep place because that's your work, but I can't imagine," he said, searching for words, "that we could get the average...Teamster, for instance...to participate in such a dialogue." It was as if he had punched me in the stomach with his words. And before I could censor my words, I blurted out a secret and the truth: "I started my work life as a Teamster." There was stunned silence. For a minute. Two minutes. Longer. Then a quiet voice from the back of the room said, "I think I just adjusted my mental model."

Months later, I was flying home from a long stretch on the road. The big jet was full. I'd been upgraded to first class where the only empty seat was next to me. The wind was so strong that it was rocking the big plane still at the gate. The last passenger strode on board and slid past me into the window seat on my left. He was a big scruffy man, tattooed, with an unruly beard. The flight attendant asked if he'd like anything to drink "A double whiskey," he said. "I hate to fly." It was I thought to myself, going to be a long ride home. As we lifted off in the great shaking gusts of wind, he regaled me loudly with stories of how the rich were soaking life out of the working poor and why the unions (of which he was a representative) were being decimated by the efforts of the rich to get the little guys. It was getting very cool in

∞

first class. Then he was quiet and so was I. "Look down there," he said, pointing out the window. "Isn't it beautiful? Sometimes I think how it must have looked thousands of years ago to those who lived here. When I go on vacations with my family, I drive them nuts, because I like to go to cemeteries where great people have been buried and sit next to their tombstones and think what they have done for us, for all of us." Another long silence and as we approach Washington he says, "It really is beautiful down there. You know, we're funny, we human beings. We buy all those lottery tickets in hopes that some day we will win the big prize and what we don't realize is that we won the prize the day we were born."

∞

Stop it

Stop it right now.
Stop all the judging, planning,
Stern admonishments
About the task to come.
Just stop it.

For just one moment
Could we breathe it in—
The little victory
Of our work danced
With effortless integrity?

For just one moment
Could we celebrate
And hug each other gleefully
And laugh, and throw a hat
High over head?

For just one moment
Could we close our eyes
In silence, savoring the joy
Of something difficult and beautiful,
Attempted? Done.

For just one moment could we feel
The deep connection
Built in laboring together,
And in caring for the work
And for each other?

The time will come, too soon,
To plan the next thing,
And to judge the last.

∞

Seconds

She sells the perfect ones,
The cups and bowls without
A flaw, the ones that
With a potter's eye and hand
She knows will likely never
Chip nor break,
Will stand the heat and cold,
Weather a thousand washings
And remain as new.

The seconds?
Those she keeps and uses,
Lives with day to day.
Some have a flaw
That even I can see;
Others look perfect
To my untrained eye,
But she's aware
They won't withstand
The challenge
Of a stranger's
Daily use.

"Incomplete ideas" she calls
The ones she keeps
Just for herself.
"Unfinished thoughts,"
The seconds, plates and bowls,
Not flawed but incomplete.

Perhaps it's true for
All of us who craft a thing,
Who write a poem,
Build a boat,
Shape an idea
Or an enterprise

The perfect ones,
The ones that work,
We sell or give away.
We move beyond them.
On to something new.
They pass out of our minds.

The yet unfinished thoughts
Ideas incomplete,
Things that won't work,
We look at every day.
We live more with the
Flaws of craft
Than with its perfect form.

Perhaps that's why
It's difficult to see
The grace of our own artistry,
To bring to mind the gifts
We've shipped away from us,
To recollect the beauty of
A plate that someone
Else can touch
From day to day,
While we ourselves
Thrice daily
Take our nourishment
From pieces that
We know are flawed.

∞

Appreciative Inquiry; a Reflective Process for Change

Appreciative Inquiry, an approach to leadership and change is associated with the work of David Cooperrider. It is probably one of the most important innovations in the field of leadership and organizational development over the past several decades.

It offers leaders and teams a pathway toward change that is energizing and creative. And it helps us move beyond trying to fix problems as a way to create a better world. Instead it helps us focus our attention on what it is that we want to create (the desired state), and the circumstances under which that desired state already exists.

Appreciative Inquiry operates on the premise that what we pay attention to grows. Attention grows and amplifies what it focuses on. This is particularly true of leadership attention. Thus if we pay attention to problems, even to fix them, we amplify them. There is more leverage (while doing minimal necessary fixing of what doesn't work) in paying attention to what it is that we want and thereby amplifying and growing it. That notion is the source of the word "appreciative" in Appreciative Inquiry—the theory is based on the power of appreciation as a force for amplifying and growing what we want.

The "inquiry" in Appreciative Inquiry points us toward the power of inquiry in helping people identify the circumstances under which they have already experienced, or are experiencing, the desired state. For instance, if you are seeking more honest dialogue in the organization, you would have people "inquire" with each other about times when there was more honest dialogue: "When was a time that you found yourself in a powerfully honest dialogue about what matters? What did you

∞

do that contributed to that dialogue? What did others do that made it possible? What else in the context was helpful?" This process of inquiry (in the form of interviews, a check-in, or reflective writing) about the desired state, helps people pull to consciousness the reality and possibility of what they want, and to detail how it has been achieved.

Bringing the reality to a conscious level moves us past our anxiety about barriers that stand in our way, and helps us tap the power of what we want. It gives us energy and perspective, as well as data on how to accomplish what we want. Then later we can turn, if necessary, to reducing barriers.

So leaders utilize the power of appreciative inquiry when they ask when the desired state is showing up, and also when they create processes where others engage in that inquiry. They can also tap the power of appreciative inquiry by being very intentional about where they place their attention.

The leadership "attention" practice that can help shift a system from problem fixing and complaining toward appreciating and changing has four steps that are practiced by the leader, and others, in this order:

1. Notice the presence of what you want whenever it shows up. No matter how small. No matter how brief. No matter where it shows up. Just notice it and appreciate it internally. You might say to yourself, "Well what do you know, Stella just did a remarkable job on that three minute presentation."

2. Appreciate the desired state verbally to the other person, or the group. You would say to Stella, "The presentation that you did had wonderful clarity and powerful images; it's just exactly what we dream of happening around here."

∞

3. Get a public "blessing" of the desired state—have someone who is in a more powerful role, or who is a respected expert, publicly praise the accomplishment. That adds more fuel to the positive fires. You might get the CEO to mention the power of the presentation and its impact on the creativity of the organization.

4. Shower the effort with resources—really shine a light on it, give it space, time, equipment–anything at all that will help it grow. You might suggest that Stella and colleagues take some time to expand the notions of the presentation into a format that could be incorporated into the annual report, and provide resources of specialized soft-ware to accomplish that.

∞

I wonder

I wonder
What this day
Will bring
In its unfolding.
Now it begins,
For me,
Like the
Unwrapping
Of an
Unexpected
Gift.

∞

A Thin Film

When I
Stare
At the
Moon
Through my
Slightly
Dirty windows,
It seems
To glow.

There is
Pleasure
In the
Softening halo
Of a
Thin film
Of illusion.

∞

Loon Song

Sometimes a solitary loon floats
On the glassy pond at dawn
Just off the cabin's point
In silence.

Across the pond
Another loon cries out.
Then silence.
This one makes no answer.
Listens. Silent. Dives. Appears.
Then floats, head turned.

Why, thus, no answer?
Was the question
To another listener?
Or was it so compelling
That no answer can be made?
Or in the world of loons is
Silence the response of choice,
Of deep respect?

Would that as friends and colleagues
We could recognize that voice,
And listen to the call in silence,
Head turned toward the call,
In pensive silence,
Wondering, respectful.

∞

Balancing Advocacy and Inquiry by Shifting to Questions and Increasing Ones Listening.

Since many leaders and leadership teams err on the side of advocacy, argument and statement, it often takes intention to shift to inquiry. Here is some guidance on how to make that shift so that inquiry and advocacy can be more balanced.

Use questions designed to draw out the thinking and feeling of the other:

> Ask questions that only the other person, alone, of all people in the universe, can answer: "When did you first begin to be interested in this?" "What experience has most shaped your perspective on this topic?"

> Ask questions for which you have no possible idea of the answer, questions for which you have no theory: "If you asked your best friend what to do in this situation, what would she say?"

> Ask questions that come from a compassionate curiosity about the other's experience, about how they think and how they feel: "Why is this causing you so much discomfort? How has it changed over time?"

Listen in a way that increases the engagement of the other:

> Listen for information not confirmation.

> Listen with wonder. Curiosity.

∞

See how completely you can let go of your tendency to
analyze or to prepare an answer. Simply absorb what is
said. Be present to what you are hearing.

Listen as if you didn't have a care in the world and had no
responsibility to analyze, act, react or respond, as if you
were absorbed in a good movie. Remember that listening
and waiting to talk are not the same thing.

Lunch with Alice

He's leaving
The Academy,
He told the Dean.

It seems
He wants
To linger longer
Over lunch
With Alice,
His beloved.

World-renowned
For his intellect,
The Nobel prize in hand,
He's listening
To his heart.

∞

Living a Healthy Life in the Midst of Change

I often feel my life is in recurring bouts of turmoil. And sometimes I am wise enough to realize I'm not alone in that. I remember asking a colleague in Detroit what had been happening in his life over the previous four months, since I'd seen him: "Let's see," he said. "Since we were last together, the parent company spun off 78,000 of us into a new separate enterprise. We reorganized. I have had two new bosses, but right now I don't know who my new boss will be. I have a new job and there isn't anyone to take over my old job yet. I moved my family back here from Italy, built a new house and had back surgery. I'm fine."

How in the world can we maintain healthy lives in the midst of the changes, uncertainty and chaos that are often visited upon us? And if we can figure out how to do it ourselves, how do we operate in the midst of systems and organizations where others aren't operating the same way?

Over the years, my life and the wisdom of those in organizations with whom I work have helped me discern what I believe to be several critical disciplines, a set of natural steps that can increasingly create space for a more balanced, healthy life, no matter what the world throws at us. Although these are practices we undertake on our own, they seem to increase the probability that those around us will develop similar practices (or we will be attracted toward people who live by these practices) so that over time, the teams and work communities of which we are a part will come to work in these ways.

Live by Vision.

I begin by deepening my own sense of purpose, of vision. What is it I want to create with my life and work? Forget the idea that

∞

someone won't let me do it. My challenge is to get clear about why I think I am in the world, and how I wish to make it a better place by stewardship of my gifts. To test the integrity of my vision, I put thoughts on paper and share them with others who know me and my work.

Hold to integrity.

Sometimes my own sense of integrity gets blurred in the political correctness of an organization, by my own politeness, by the needs of others, or by the tidal waves of change. How can I stay centered in the midst of all this? I practice beginning each day, and each piece of work by asking myself, "What do I want to make sure happens no matter what? What do I want to model and represent no matter what? What am I dedicated to, from which no one can deter me, no matter what?"

The very idea of "no matter what's" helps to keep me on track. It does not mean that I am unyielding or inflexible; it means I practice living by my "essentials."

Speak the truth.

I practice speaking my own truth (a combination of my perspective, feelings and thinking) even when it feels risky. I invite and welcome the truth of others and invite them into my dilemmas.

In a dialogue, a group of engineers decide that the only thing that keeps us from speaking our perspective is fear—fear of being wrong, of retribution, of not being liked, of not being polite, of being outcast. Yet when I think of my perspective as a contribution that only I can make—something I owe to the organization or to those I care about—I cease to withhold it out of fear that it will not be valued. Silence can be costly, and discounting a troublesome perspective can lead to disaster.

∞

Steward your energy.

I notice whatever makes me feel fully alive and present and then I turn my attention toward it. I go there with my life. Once at a particularly difficult time in my life (my father was dying, my family was moving, I hated my boss and the feeling seemed mutual, my career was taking a turn into terra incognita), in an act of intuition and desperation, I pulled out a sheet of paper and wrote at the top: "People who draw my best energies." Just seeing their names made me feel better. I put the paper away and forgot about it. Months later I ran across it and was stunned to realize I was now in contact with everyone on that list, and working with most of them. I had been stuck but now I was free.

Practice courage.

Some folks may be born courageous, but I am not one of them. For me, courage is an ongoing practice that takes persistence. It is a practice that is especially helpful in the face of change, when our natural human fears of failure, chaos, loss, scarcity and isolation rise to the fore. Courage isn't fearlessness; it is acknowledging our fears and anxiety, taking a deep breath and, instead of following our usual fear response, choosing a response path that is healthier for us, for those we care about, and for the organization. That healthier path is often one of engagement, moving toward the point of fear, and using the power of inquiry to find a path through the issue that is so fearsome.

Take natural steps forward.

I do my best to practice these approaches in a consistent natural way. I use plain English to describe them so they are accessible to those who inquire about them. I am forthcoming about my reasons for being committed to them, but I avoid marketing them or promoting them as some new dogma. I do my best to live them into being.

∞

Be tolerant.

I recognize that, being human, I will have days when my old
habits catch me and others by surprise, yet I am patient with
myself. I remember the words of an insurance executive
describing how leaders must behave to engage the workforce in
times of change: "It's not that some folks get this stuff and others
don't. I get it. I lose it. I get it back. I forget it. You remind me. I
get it back again." I learn to be tolerant of my own humanness
and I extend the same tolerance to others.

Make time for reflection.

I make time for reflection to trace the shifts in my thinking. These
shifts in thinking, though dizzying, are the footprints of my
learning. I know that different people reflect and learn from
experience in different ways. In order to give people private space
for reflection, when I work with groups I provide them with
journals, or notebooks, which act as a structure for private
reflection. One young engineer told me: "I turned the page and
there was this remarkable quote. I thought about what it said and
I found myself writing things I didn't know I knew. Funniest
thing."

Increase your awareness.

We are all superbly trained to make judgments and take actions.
Fast. "A bias for action," we say of ourselves. Yet if we are to
make progress in living and working in these more effective ways,
we need a bias for awareness, for noticing, for observing without
judgment or analysis. I simply collect data by noticing what I am
seeing, experiencing, feeling, thinking. Only then do I tell myself
a story about what is going on. We all have favorite stories.
Sometimes we aren't even aware of them or of the data points that
trigger us to act on them. Increasing our awareness helps us

∞

explore whether our stories serve us, or the truth, well. We need to keep asking about ideas that don't work that we repeat to ourselves. Through awareness we begin to replace those ideas that don't reflect reality with a more grounded conscious awareness.

Express appreciation.

Appreciation nourishes the things we want. It is a disciplined capacity to notice and acknowledge the presence of the things for which we most yearn—the things we wish to create with our lives. It requires discerning things in incomplete states, in seed states, and in places we didn't ask for them (and sometimes don't want them). Appreciation encourages, amplifies, and nourishes what we want. I think of appreciation as watering seeds that have been planted by our vision.

In sum, core principles for a healthy life in the midst of ambiguity and change:

- Respect for the essence and integrity of the human spirit;
- Commitment to skilled, disciplined, courageous conversation about what matters most;
- Awareness of how my ways of thinking and feeling shape my experience;
- The need to take action in the world;
- Realization that the change we seek starts within us in some form of inner discipline;
- Commitment to a vision-oriented, values-shaped life.
- Pursuit of truth and joy;
- Awareness and experience of the vitality of life.

∞

Stories

When the stories
Begin and we listen,
Really listen
To each other,
We begin
To notice
That we are not
Quite so much the same
As we had thought,
At least
Not in the ways
We thought.
And we are not
So different as we thought,
At least not in the ways
We thought.
And like some
Big old family
Full of odd relatives,
We are all kin,
Befuddled
And beloved.

∞

Check In and Check Out

What is "check-in" ?
It is a way to begin work or a meeting with each person, in turn, "checking in" by speaking briefly.

Why do "check-in"?
It gets each person's voice into the conversation. It helps each person be present. It allows each individual to talk about what's on their mind, to disclose information that is important to them. It can provide important information about what is going on with individuals so others aren't making assumptions about why someone is quiet, or distracted. It can make public information about the particular perspectives, experiences and skills that individuals bring to the work. That can jump-start effective team dynamics.

How do you do "check-in"?
- Put the check-in question on newsprint;
- Ask who wants to start;
- Give the speaker an object (a koosh ball is handy as the object) that signals that one person is speaking and all other people are listening. The person speaks until finished. Their words stand alone and do not require any response. No "cross chat" or response allowed;
- Each speaker passes the koosh to the next person who signals they wish to speak. Allow some silence between check-ins. Continue until everyone has spoken, or has indicated a "pass."

What's a good check-in question?
A good check-in question has these qualities: 1) anyone can come up with an answer without worrying about being second-guessed by somebody else; 2) it surfaces fresh in-the-moment thinking;

∞

3) the answer is absolutely unique to the speaker. The best questions are two-parters, the first part draws out what the person is sure of, the second part what they are confused about. That creates the largest space for dialogue, by creating a field for both advocacy (what I know) and inquiry (what I wonder about). An example: "What do you know with reasonable certainty about this work we are doing together, and what is your biggest question?"

Examples of questions that work:
- What's on your mind coming into our work together?
- What series of events or choice points or steppingstones have brought you here today?
- What do you want to make sure happens in our work today, no matter what?
- What is your greatest hope about our work together, and what is your biggest fear?
- What about this work matters most to you?

What about "check-out"? Check out is a parallel process at the end of the work. Without a check-out people assume everybody else is thinking like they are at the end of the meeting. Or they make assumptions about where people are. It is a way to actually get data rather than make assumptions. People can check out with
- A single word that describes your state of mind as we end the work together;
- "What do your take away from today's work?"
- What are you most certain of? What is your biggest question?
- A two part check-out that is the most powerful after extended work together: What do you take away from this work together, and what do you choose to leave behind because it no longer serves you, in order to move forward in the work?

∞

The Beauty of the Broken

The beauty
Of the broken
And irregular
Is clear
With seashells—
Why not so
With one another?

∞

Trust

Trust rises and falls
Like a tide.
See now it ebbs,
The shoals are visible,
The waves break
Far from shore.
Then, as is ever true,
We glance away,
Distracted by
Some beauty,
And fail to notice
That the waves upon the sand
Are now
Much closer to our feet.
The tide
Is coming in again.
Who or what
Makes it thus,
This breathing in and out
Of universe,
This feeling love
Give way to fear
And then to love
Again?
How do I,
Losing faith in you
Or me,
Wait for the tide
To do its work,
Turning,
To then
Transform our world?

∞

Assessment of Personal Leadership Practices

For each of the practices below, please rate your current level of discipline/practice, as you see it, "1 -5" with "1" being low and "5" being high. This is personal work for you. You may find it opens important conversation with yourself and even eventually with others.

Practices	1	2	3	4	5
Vision: a clear articulated sense of compelling positive personal vision strong enough to sustain a life-time contribution					
Centering: the capacity to stay centered, (balanced, calm, at ones personal best) and to return to a centered place in the midst of surprise and or challenge, particularly in the presence of paradox, where one must honor two seemingly competing truths.					
Mental Awareness: practices which help one stay aware of the inner mental, and conceptual processes. Noting assumptions and setting them aside.					
Mental Flexibility: practices which help one stretch one's mental frames					
Focus: practices which help one maintain attention in the midst of mental and emotional distractions					
Norms: a clear sense of the personal "ethic" which you hold no matter what. The ability to help collectives create sustaining norms					
Truth-Speaking: the capacity for personal authentic voice, Perspective					
Listening: the capacity to listen with curiosity, wondering, even when what is being heard is not necessary welcome nor expected nor coming from a favorite source					
Creativity: practices which enhance creativity of thinking and response including art, music, poetry, photography, movement and writing					
Awareness of Perceptive Processes: Awareness of blind spots, attention to increasing the range of perceptive channels, and to increased acuity in each					

∞

Strategy for Personal Leadership Practices

For each of the practices below, please note how you currently achieve each and ideas for strengthening your practice.

Practices	Strategies I use or that I might adopt
Vision: a clear articulated sense of compelling positive personal vision strong enough to sustain a life-time contribution	
Centering: the capacity to stay centered, (balanced, calm, at ones personal best) and to return to a centered place in the midst of surprise and or challenge, particularly in the presence of paradox, where one must honor two seemingly competing truths	
Mental Awareness: practices which help one stay aware of the inner mental, and conceptual processes. Noting assumptions and setting them aside.	
Focus: practices which help one maintain attention in the midst of mental and emotional distractions	
Mental Flexibility: practices which help one stretch one's mental frames	
Norms: a clear sense of the personal "ethic" which you hold no matter what. The ability to help collectives create sustaining norms	
Creativity: practices which enhance creativity of thinking and response including art, music, poetry, photography, movement and writing	
Truth-Speaking: the capacity for personal authentic voice, perspective	
Listening: the capacity to listen with curiosity, wondering, even when what is being heard is not necessary welcome nor expected nor coming from a favorite source	
Awareness of Perceptive Processes: Awareness of blind spots, attention to increasing the range of perceptive channels, and to increased acuity in each	

The Pizza Came

The pizza came
But not the rental chairs.
So the tough issues
They were so upset about,
Had to be talked about
One at a time
With folks sitting
Upon the floor,
Informal, pow-wow style,
Listening to one another.
Eating pizza.
Even laughing
Now and then.
They'll meet again
Like that
In two more weeks.
They've found
A whole new world
Together.
If the chairs had come
And not the pizza,
They would have been
In an entirely
Different place.
Providence moves
In strange ways.

∞

Some Days

Some days
You see the depth
Of distant hills
Because the light
Is touching them
Just so—
And other moments
That detail, perspective,
Is completely lost to view,
And there is nothing
You can do
But just recall
What you've already seen,
Try to remember the detail.
It's the condition
Of the light
That changes all.

∞

Touchstones

Ideas that increase the likelihood of our working together productively:

1) **Come to the work with 100% of the self.** Set aside the usual distractions of phone mail, e-mail, things undone from yesterday, things to do tomorrow. Bring all of yourself to the work, not just the parts of yourself and your experience that would be obviously relevant to this work. Be 100% present here.

2) **Let the beauty we love be what we do.** Think of all the things you value and enjoy in life. Bring them with you in your peripheral vision. Bring their richness along as resources. Consider what they have to teach us about the dilemmas we are exploring today. Rumi says it best:

> Today, like every other day, we wake up empty
> and frightened. Don't open the door to the study
> and begin reading. Take down a musical instrument.
>
> Let the beauty we love be what we do.
> There are hundreds of ways to kneel and kiss the ground.

3) **Presume welcome and extend welcome.** We all learn most effectively in spaces which welcome us. Therefore we have a responsibility to welcome each other to this place and this work and to presume that we are being welcomed, as well.

4) **Nose into inquiry.** When we feel challenged or confused, switch from saying to asking, from advocating to inquiry,

∞

from knowing to wondering, from stating to questioning. Like a canoe trying to make headway up a lake in the wind, nose straight into the wind, head into inquiry. When it's hard, turn to wonder.

5) **Consider that it is possible to emerge from the conversation refreshed, wondering, curious, surprised.** Expect that our time together can provide for renewal, refreshment, helpful perspectives on the work at hand. Our work is not about more "to-do" but rather more effortless ways to do that which we must do.

∞

About the author

Judy Sorum Brown is a leadership educator, author, poet and speaker whose work revolves around the themes of leadership, transformation, change, dialogue and creativity. She is particularly interested in the inner dimensions of leadership and the roots of authenticity. She teaches Leadership for the Public Good at the Graduate School of Public Policy at the University of Maryland where she is affiliated with the James MacGregor Burns Academy of Leadership. Her other books include *The Choice,* a book about learning, loss and renewal, and her collection of poetry *The Sea Accepts all Rivers.*

She and her husband David live in the Washington, D.C area.

She can be reached at JudyBrown@aol.com or via her website at www.JudySorumBrown.com.

∞

258

Bibliography

Angelou, Maya. (1969). I *Know Why the Caged Bird Sings.* New York: Random House

Argyris, Chris. "Double Loop Learning in Organizations." *Harvard Business Review,* September-October 1977

Argyris, Chris. "Teaching Smart People How to Learn." *Harvard Business Review,* May-June1991.

Bennett-Goleman, Tara. (2001). *Emotional Alchemy.* NY: Harmony Books.

Bettleheim, Bruno. (1988). *The Uses of Enchantment.* New York: Vintage Books.

Bly, Robert. (1992). *Iron John.* New York: Vintage Books.

Bly, Robert. (1997). *Morning Poems.* New York: HarperCollins.

Bohm, David. (1990). "On Dialogue." Material edited from a meeting November 6, 1989. P.O. Box 1452, Ojai, CA 93023.

Bok, Sissela. (1978). *Lying.* New York: Vintage Books.

Boulding, Kenneth (1995) *Sonnets from Later Life, 1981-1993.* Pendle Hill.

Boulding, Kenneth (April 1, 1985) *The World as a Total System.* Sage Publications, Inc.

Bridges, William. (1980). *Transitions; Making Sense of Life's Changes.* New York: Addison-Wesley.

Brown, Juanita with David Issacs and the World Café Community. (2005) *The World Café; Shaping Our Futures Through Conversations that Matter.* San Francisco: Berrett-Koehler Publishers, Inc.

∞

Brown, Judy. (1995). *The Choice: Seasons of Loss and Renewals After a Father's Decision to Die.* Berkeley, CA: Conari Press.

Brown, Judy. (1995) "Dialogue: Capacities and Stories." *Learning Organizations: Developing Cultures for Tomorrow's Workplace.* Portland, Oregon: Productivity Press.

Brown, Judy. (2000) *The Sea Accepts all Rivers and other poems.* Alexandria, VA: Miles River Press.

Brownowski, Jacob. (1978). *The Origins of Knowledge and Imagination.* Connecticut: Yale University.

Bryner, Andy and Markova, Dawna. (1996). *An Unused Intelligence: Physical Thinking for 21st Century Leadership.* Berkeley, CA: Conari Press.

Cameron, Julia. (1992). *The Artist's Way: A Spiritual Path to Higher Creativity.* New York: Jeremy P. Tarcher/Perigee

Campbell, Joseph. (1972). *Myths to Live By.* New York: Bantam Books.

Campbell, Joseph. (1949). *The Hero with a Thousand Faces.* New Jersey: Princeton University Press.

Capra, Fritjof. (1975). *The Tao of Physics.* New York: Bantam Books.

Capra, Fritjof. (1988). *The Turning Point.* New York: Bantam Books.

Cooperrider, D.L. and D. Whitney. (1999) *Appreciative Inquiry* San Francisco: Berrett-Koehler.

Daly, Herman E. and Cobb, Jr., John B. (1989, 1994). *For the Common Good: Redirecting the Economy toward Community, the Environment, and Sustainable Future.* Boston: Beacon Press.

Darwin, Charles. (1892). *The autobiography of Charles Darwin and selected letters.* New York: Dover Publications Inc.

∞

Drucker, Peter F. "Managing Oneself." *Harvard Business Review* March-April 1999.

Einstein, Albert. (1961). *Relativity – the special and the general theory*. New York: Crown Publishers.

Eiseley, Loren. (1973).*The Man who Saw through Time*. New York: Charles Scribner's Sons.

Franck, Frederick. (1973). *The Zen of Seeing: Seeing/Drawing as Meditation*. New York: Vintage Books.

Frankl, Viktor E. (1977). *Man's Search for Meaning*. New York: Simon & Schuster, Inc.

Frenier, C.R. (1966) *Business and the Feminine Principle: The Untapped Resource*. Woburn, MA: Butterworth-Heinemann Publishers.

Gardner, John W. (2003). *Living, Leading, and the American Dream*. Edited by Francesca Gardner. San Francisco: Jossey-Bass; A Wiley Imprint.

Gardner, John W. "Personal Renewal." Delivered to the Marriott Executive Development Program at The Aspen Institute on September 13, 1990.

Gardner, John W. (1990). *On Leadership*. New York: The Free Press.

Gardner, John W. (1983). *Self Renewal: The Individual and the Innovative Society*. New York: W. W. Norton & Co.

Gelb, M.J (1998). *How to Think Like Leonardo da Vinci*. New York: Dell Publishing,

Gilligan, Carol. (1982). *In a Different Voice*. Cambridge, MA: Harvard University Press.

Gleick, James. (1987). *Chaos*. New York: Penguin Books.

∞

Goleman, Daniel, McKee, Annie and Boyatzis, Richard E. (2002). *Primal Leadership: Realizing the Power of Emotional Intelligence.* Boston, MA: Harvard Business School Press.

Hawking, Stephen W. (1988). *A Brief History of Time.* New York: Bantam Books.

Heifetz, Ronald A. and Linsky, Marty. (2002). *Leadership on the Line: Staying Alive through the Dangers of Leading.* Boston, MA: Harvard Business School Press.

Heifetz, Ronald A. (1994). *Leadership Without Easy Answers.* Cambridge, MA: Belknapp Press of Harvard University Press.

Hesselbein, Frances. (2002). *Hesselbein on Leadership.* San Francisco, CA: Jossey-Bass Inc.

Hughes, Richard L, Ginnett, Robert C. and Curphy, Gordon J. (1993 & 1996). *Leadership: Enhancing the Lessons of Experience.* Boston, Massachusetts: Irwin.

Intrator, Sam M. and Megan Scribner, Editors (2003) *Teaching with Fire: Poetry that Sustains the Courage to Teach.* San Francisco, CA: Jossey-Bass.

Jones, Michael. (1995). *Creating an Imaginative Life.* Berkeley, CA: Conari Press.

Kegan, Robert and Lahey, Lisa Laskow. (2001) *How the Way We Talk Can Change the Way We Work: Seven Languages for Transformation.* San Francisco: Jossey-Bass.

Keller, Evelyn Fox. (1985). *Reflections on Gender and Science.* New Haven: Yale University Press.

Keillor, Garrison (2003) *Good Poems.* New York, Penguin Books.

Keynes, John Maynard (1964) *The General Theory of Employment, Interest, and Money.* New York, Harcourt, Brace and World.

∞

King, Martin Luther. "Letter from Birmingham City Jail." (Written to his Fellow Clergymen in 1963). Christian Century. 80, June 12, 1963, 767-773.

Kolb, David A. 1984. *Experiential Learning: Experience as the Source of Learning and Development.* Prentice-Hall, Inc., Englewood Cliffs, N.J.

Kuhn, Thomas S. (1970). *The Structure of Scientific Revolutions.* Chicago: The University of Chicago Press.

Losada, Marcial F. and Heaphy, Emily. "The Role of Positivity and Connectivity in the Performance of Business Teams: A Nonlinear Dynamical Model." *American Behavioral Scientist* (February 2004), Vol. 47, No. 6, pp. 740-765.

Markova, Dawna. (1994) *No Enemies Within.* Berkeley, CA. Conari Press.

Markova, Dawna. (2000). *I Will Not Die an Unlived Life: Reclaiming Purpose and Passion.* Berkeley, CA: Conari Press.

Maturana, Humberto R. and Varela, Francisco. (1992). *The Tree of Knowledge: The Biological Roots of Human Understanding.* Boston, MA: Shambhala.

Mayeroff, Milton. (1972). *On Caring.* New York: Harper & Row.

Mintzberg, Henry. (1987). "Crafting Strategy." *Harvard Business Review,* 65(4), 66-77.

Myers, Isabel Briggs & Myers, Peter B. (1980). *Gifts Differing.* Palo Alto, CA: Consulting Psychologists Press, Inc.

Neustadt, Richard E. and May, Ernest R. (1986). *Thinking in Time: The Uses of History for Decision-Makers.* New York: The Free Press.

Owen, H (1997). *Expanding Our Now: The Story of Open Space Technology* San Francisco: Berrett-Koehler Publishers.

∞

Palmer, Parker J. (1998). *The Courage to Teach*. San Francisco, CA: Jossey-Bass Inc.

Palmer, Parker J. "Leading From Within." Delivered to the Meridian Street United Methodist Church in Indiana on March 23, 1990. Available from Potter's House Book Service, 1658 Columbia Road NW, Washington DC 20009.

Palmer, Parker J. (2000). *Let Your Life Speak: Listening for the Voice of Vocation*. San Francisco, CA: Jossey-Bass Inc.

Pearson, Carol. (1998). *The Hero Within*. New York: HarperCollins.

Perry, William G., Jr. (1968). *Forms of Intellectual and Ethical Development in the College Years*. New York: Holt, Rinehart and Winston, Inc.

Prigogine, Iilya & Stengers, Isabelle. (1984). *Order Out of Chaos*. New York: Bantam Books.

Progoff, Ira. (1975). *At a Journal Workshop*. New York: Dialogue House Library.

Rockwell, I. (2002). *The Five Wisdom Energies: A Buddhist Way of Understanding Personalities, Emotions, and Relationships* (Boston: Shambhala Institute.

Rumi (1984) *Open Secret* .Putney, Vermont. Threshold Books.

Schwartz, P. (1991)*The Art of the Long View* New York: Doubleday.

Senge, Peter, Scharmer, C. Otto, Jaworski, Joseph, Flowers, Betty Sue. (2004). *Presence: Human Purpose and the Field of the Future*. Cambridge, MA: The Society for Organizational Learning.

Senge, Peter M. (1990). *The Fifth Discipline*. New York: Doubleday.

∞

Senge, Peter M., Roberts, Charlotte., Ross, Richard B., Smith, Bryan J., and Kleiner, Art. (1994). *The Fifth Discipline Fieldbook: Strategies And Tools For Building A Learning Organization.* New York: Currency/Doubleday,

Shakespeare, William. (1974). G. Blakemore Evans Harvard University (Textual Editor), *The Riverside Shakespeare.* Boston: Houghton Mifflin Company.

Snow, C. P. (1969). *Two Cultures: and a Second Look.* New York: Cambridge University Press.

Spencer, Paula Underwood. (1983). *Who Speaks for Wolf.* Austin: Tribe of Two Press.

Stafford, W. *Learning to Live in the World* (New York: Harcourt Brace & Co., 1994).

Stone, Douglas. Et al. (1999). *Difficult Conversations.* New York: Penguin Books.

Tannen, Deborah. (1990). *You Just Don't Understand.* New York: William Morrow and Company.

Tannen, Deborah. (1994). *Talking from 9 to 5.* New York: William Morrow and Company.

Thomas, Lewis. (1980). *The Lives of a Cell.* New York: Bantam Books.

Underwood, Paula. (1993). *The Walking People: A Native American Oral History.* Austin: Tribe of Two Press.

Underwood, Paula. (1994). *Three Strands in the Braid.* Austin, TX: Tribe of Two Press.

Vaill, Peter B. (1990). *Managing as a Performing Art.* San Francisco: Jossey-Bass Publishers.

∞

Vaill, Peter B. (1996). *Learning as a Way of Being: Strategies for Survival in a World of Permanent White Water.* San Francisco: Jossey-Bass Publishers.

Watson, James D. (1968). *The Double Helix* . New York: Atheneum Publishers.

Weisbord, Marvin R. (1987). *Productive Workplaces.* San Francisco: Jossey-Bass.

Wheatley, Margaret J. (1992). *Leadership and the New Science.* San Francisco: Berrett-Koehler Publishers, Inc.

Wheatley, Margaret J. and Kellner-Rogers, Myron. (1996). *A SimplerWay.* San Francisco: Berrett-Koehler Publishers.

Wheatley, Margaret J. (2002). *Turning to One Another: Simple Conversations to Restore Hope to the Future.* San Francisco: Berrett-Koehler Publishers, Inc.

Yankelovich, Daniel. (1999). *The Magic of Dialogue..* New York: Simon & Schuster.

∞

266

VIDEO/FILM/DVD.

Charthouse Learning Corporation. Barker, Joel Arthur (Director). (1990). *Discovering the Future Series – The Business of Paradigms*. [Video]. Burnsville, MN: Charthouse Learning Corporation.

Carreras, Domingo, Pavarotti with Mehta. (1990). Compact disc and video. *The Three Tenors In Concert: Performed Terme di Caracalla, Roma on 7 July 1990*. London, England: The Decca Record Company, Limited.

Hott, Lawrence and Lewis, Tom. (1997) *Divided Highways: The Interstates and the Transformation of American Life*. Video. Films for the Humanities and Sciences, Box 2053, Princeton NJ 08543-2053.

John Gardner; Uncommon American, Richard Dreyfuss narrator. Video.

Shackleton's Antarctic Adventure; The Greatest Survival Story of all Time. (2002) Kevin Spacey narrator. DVD. White Mountain Films and NOVA/WGBH Boston.

∞

Printed in the United States
114771LV00003B/91/A